C++ Distilled

A Concise ANSI/ISO
Reference and
Style Guide

C++ Distilled

A Concise ANSI/ISO Reference and Style Guide

Ira Pohl

University of California
Santa Cruz

ADDISON-WESLEY

An imprint of Addison Wesley Longman, Inc.

Reading, Massachusetts • Harlow, England • Menlo Park, California
Berkeley, California • Don Mills, Ontario • Sydney
Bonn • Amsterdam • Tokyo • Mexico City

Many of the designations used by manufacturers and sellers to distinguish their products are claimed as trademarks. Where those designations appear in this book and Addison Wesley Longman, Inc. was aware of a trademark claim, the designations have been printed with initial capital letters or all capital letters.

The authors and publishers have taken care in preparation of this book, but make no expressed or implied warranty of any kind and assume no responsibility for errors or omissions. No liability is assumed for incidental or consequential damages in connection with or arising out of the use of the information or programs contained herein.

The publisher offers discounts on this book when ordered in quantity for special sales. For more information, please contact:

Corporate & Professional Publishing Group
Addison Wesley Longman, Inc.
One Jacob Way
Reading, Massachusetts 01867

Library of Congress Cataloging-in-Publication Data
Pohl, Ira

C++ distilled: a consise ANSI/ISO reference and sytle guide / by Ira Pohl.
p. cm.
Includes bibliographical references and index.
ISBN 0-201-69587-1 (pbk. : alk. paper)
1. C++ (Computer program language) I. Title.
QA76.73.C153P6   1997
005.13'3—dc21   96-29545
                                                            CIP

Text design by Wilson Graphics & Design (Kenneth J. Wilson)
Text printed on recycled and acid-free paper

ISBN 0-201-69587-1
1 2 3 4 5 6 7 8 9-MA-99989796
First printing, November 1996

Preface

C++ Distilled: A Concise ANSI/ISO Reference and Style Guide is a companion volume for the student or professional programmer who uses ANSI C++, including the I/O, and STL library. It supplements and brings up-to-date existing literature.

This book is a concise road map and style guide to C++. It selectively previews the proposed ANSI standard C++ language and includes many programming tips. It is easily used with any C++ programming book (see Chapter 20, "References," on page 189, for a selection), but is especially suitable when used with one of the author's books, such as *Object-Oriented Programming Using C++, 2nd Edition* (reference OPUS 97).

Each section has the syntax, semantics, and examples of the language element. There are style and programming tips at the end of most sections. Examples have a consistent professional style to be mimicked by programmers.

This book is a distillation of the ANSI standard, which is approximately 700 detailed technically dense pages, and rather overwhelming. Fortunately most programmers do not need such detail; indeed, many of the features are highly specialized and little used. Most programmers need to be able to quickly review some syntax or semantics they have not recently used.

C++ has had many recent additions, including STL, namespaces, RTTI, and the bool type. These can be used readily by someone already proficient in basic C++, but most books have yet to treat these topics. This book can provide a handy guide to these new constructs.

The examples both within the book are intended to exhibit good programming style. Most programming is done in my imitation of existing code and idioms. These examples use my prescriptions and programming tips ("Dr. P's Prescriptions") which are a distillation of considerable professional practice.

The Addison-Wesley web site contains the programs in this book as well as adjunct programs that illustrate the points made in the book or flesh out short pieces of programs. The programs available at the web site are introduced by their *.cpp* or *.h* names and can be obtained by referencing

www.aw.com/cseng/authors/pohl/drp/*program_name*.cpp

 **Example Program**

In file hello1.cpp

```
//Traditional first program
#include <iostream.h>

int main()
{
    cout << "HELLO WORLD!" << endl;
}
```

 Dr. P's Prescriptions: Style and Rule Tips

- Use the style found in this book.

- Be consistent with whatever style you choose.

Prescription Discussion

Style emphasizes clarity and community norms. Consistency, while the hobgoblin of small minds, is well suited to large computer codes.

Acknowledgments

This book was developed with the support of my editor J. Carter Shanklin, editorial assistant Angela Buenning, and production coordinator Pamela Yee. Thanks also to reviewers Ed Lansinger of General Motors Corporation; Henry A. Etlinger of Rochester Institute of Technology; Glen Deen of Deen Publications, Inc.; Michael Keenan of Columbus State University; and David Gregory. Most importantly, I thank Debra Dolsberry for her invaluable help in the technical editing of this book, and her careful testing of the code.

Contents

Chapter 1

Program Structure

Here is a simple first program in C++ for computing the greatest common divisor of two integers.

 **GCD Program**

In file gcd.cpp

```cpp
//Compute the greatest common divisor of two integers
//Author: Laura Pohl. version 2
//Organization: Cottage Consultants, Aptos, CA

#include  <iostream.h>        //input/output library
#include  <assert.h>          //for errors

int gcd(int m, int n)         //function definition
{                             //block
   int  r;                    //declaration of remainder

   while (n != 0) {           //not equal
      r = m % n;              //modulos operator
      m = n;                  //assignment
      n = r;
   }                          //end while loop
   return m;                  //exit gcd with value m
}
```

```
int main()
{
    int g, x, y;

    cout << "\nGreatest Common Divisor";
    cout << "\nEnter two non-zero integers: ";
    cin >> x >> y;                          //input two ints
    while (x * y != 0){
        cout << "\nGCD(" << x << ", " << y << ") = "
            << (g = gcd(x, y)) << endl;
        assert(x % g == 0 && y % g ==0);    //postcondition
        cout << "\nEnter two integers: ";
        cin >> x >> y;                      //input two ints
    }
}
```

If we input two sets of integers, then zeroes to end the loop, the computer screen
shows:

```
Greatest Common Divisor
Enter two integers: 10 20
GCD(10, 20) = 10

Enter two integers: 35 14
GCD(35, 14) = 7

Enter two integers: 0 0
```

C++ Program Organization

- C++ relies on an external standard library to provide input and output (I/O). The information the program needs to use this library resides in the library file *iostream.h.*

- C++ uses a preprocessor to handle a set of directives, such as the `include` directive, to convert the program from its preprocessing form to pure C++ syntax. Directives start with the symbol #.

- A C++ program consists of declarations that may be in different files. Each function is on the external, or global, level and may not be declared in a nested manner. The files act as modules and may be separately compiled.

- The function `main()` is used as the starting point for execution of the program. It obeys the C++ rules for function declaration. It is normal practice for `main()` to implicitly return the integer value 0, indicating that the program completed normally. Other return values need to be returned explicitly and would indicate an error condition.

- The `assert` macro tests a condition for correctness, and terminates the program if the test fails.

Assuming this program resides in the file *gcd.c*, its compilation on a UNIX system using the CC command and compiling to the executable file *gcd.exe* is as follows.

```
%CC gcd.c -o gcd.exe
```

 ## Dr. P's Prescriptions: General Rules

- Dr. P's first rule of style is "Have a style."

- Kernighan and Plauger's first rule of style is "Write clearly—don't be too clever" (reference KP 74).

- Be consistent in whatever style you choose.

- Use standard libraries.

Prescription Discussion

In this book we follow the traditional C and C++ style pioneered by Bell Laboratories programmers, such as Kernighan, Ritchie and Stroustrup (references KR 88, GRAY 91, ABC 95).

Several elements of this style can be seen in the *gcd* program. Beginning and ending braces for function definitions line up under each other and under the first character of the function definition. Beginning braces after keywords, such as `do` and `while`, follow the keyword with the ending brace under the first character of that line. This style is in widespread use and makes it easy for others to read your code. The style allows us to distinguish key elements of the program visually, enhancing readability. Style should aim for clarity for both ourselves and others who need to read our code.

Cleverness by its nature is usually obscure. This is the enemy of clarity—hence Kernighan and Plauger's maxim "Write clearly—don't be too clever." Also, inconsistent style tends to obscure. Finally, existing standard libraries such as *iostream* are to be strongly preferred to idiosyncratic schemes. Since they are standard they are already understood and universally available, contributing to clarity. Standard libraries are very robust and do not require debugging and local maintenance costs.

Chapter 2

Lexical Elements

A C++ program is a sequence of characters that are collected into tokens, which comprise the basic vocabulary of the language. There are six categories of tokens: keywords, identifiers, constants, string constants, operators, and punctuators.

Characters that can be used to construct tokens are:

```
a b c d e f g h i j k l m n o p q r s t u v w x y z
A B C D E F G H I J K L M N O P Q R S T U V W X Y Z
0 1 2 3 4 5 6 7 8 9
+ - * / = () {} [] <> ' " ! # ~ % ^ & _ : ; , . ? \ |
```
White space characters such as blank and tab

In producing tokens, the compiler selects the longest string of characters that constitutes a token.

2.1 Comments

C++ has a rest-of-line comment symbol, //. The C-style comment pairs, /* */, are also available. Comments do not nest. Some examples are:

```
//Distilled C++: Addison-Wesley Program GCD

const int N = 200;        //N is number of trials
```

```
/*    *   *   *   *   *
    Programmer:    Laura M. Pohl
    Compiler:      Borland 5.0
    Modifications: 5-2-96   Stack Overflow
*    *   *   *   *   *   */
```

Except for lengthy multiline comments, the rest-of-line comment should be used. This style is easier to use and is less error prone.

2.2 Identifiers

An identifier can be one character or more. The first character must be a letter or underscore. Subsequent characters can be letters, digits, or an underscore. Though in principle identifiers can be arbitrarily long, many systems distinguish only up to the first 31 characters. Identifiers that contain a double underscore or begin with an underscore followed by an uppercase letter are reserved for use by the system.

Identifier Examples			Comments
multiWord	vector	flag_x	normal style
q213	sb3	abx1w	opaque
speed	Speed	speedy	distinct but confusing
_Sys1	__Adriver	__C__	reserved for system use
9illegal	wrong-2	il$form	illegal
typeid	this	register	keywords can't be used

2.3 Keywords

Keywords are explicitly reserved identifiers that have a strict meaning in C++. They cannot be redefined or used in other contexts. There are other keywords that are specific to implementations, such as near and far in Borland C++. The following keywords are in use in most current C++ systems.

Keywords			
asm	else	operator	throw
auto	enum	private	true
bool	explicit	protected	try
break	extern	public	typedef
case	false	register	typeid
catch	float	reinterpret_cast	typename
char	for	return	union
class	friend	short	unsigned
const	goto	signed	using
const_cast	if	sizeof	virtual
continue	inline	static	void
default	int	static_cast	volatile
delete	long	struct	wchar_t
do	mutable	switch	while
double	namespace	template	
dynamic_cast	new	this	

Dr. P's Prescriptions: Lexical Elements

- White space is free; use it for readability.

- Pick meaningful identifier names that help document a program.

- Use a standard form of initial comment.

- Use short rest-of-line comments.

- Avoid obvious comments.

- Avoid using an underscore as a starting character or a double underscore in an identifier, as many system programs use these.

- Avoid identifiers differing only by the use of upper- and lowercase letters.

- Capitalize preprocessor identifiers. Ordinary identifiers should be lowercase.

Prescription Discussion

White space aids readability. Leave white space around operators, and one statement per line for readability. Also, use one or two empty lines between major program elements, such as function and class definitions.

Meaningful identifiers are essential to a readable program. To be meaningful, an identifier should describe its use in the code. It is important to choose names that are not confusing. Though relying on case to differentiate between two names is not confusing to a compiler, it is to a person. A standard convention in the industry is to capitalize preprocessor names.

An initial comment should be standard. It should include the name of the programmer, the organization, the version, the date the program was last changed, resources needed to run the code, the chief purpose of the code, and its general form of use. An organization should adopt a standard for all its code.

Except for lengthy multiline comments, the rest-of-line comment should be used; it is easier to use and less error prone. Comments themselves should be terse but written in a clear prose style. Where possible, they should be aligned. Excessive commenting is distracting. Good choice of identifier names and clear use of structured flow of control do not need redundant comments such as "weight stores the weight of a person," or "this is a for loop."

Chapter 3

Constants

C++ has constants for each basic type. These include integer, character, and floating constants. String constants are character sequences surrounded by double quotes. There is one universal pointer constant, namely 0. Some examples follow.

Constant Examples			Comments
156	0156	0x156	integer: dec, oct, hex
156l	156u		integer: long, unsigned
'A'	'a'	'7' '\t'	character: A, a, 7, tab
3.14f	3.1415	3.14159L	floating-point constants
"A string."			string constant
true	false		bool constants

The suffixes u or U, l or L, and f or F are used to indicate unsigned, long, and float, respectively. The unsigned constants are positive numbers. The long constants have greater precision than normal. The float constants are usually less precision than an ordinary double constants.

The character constants are usually given in single quotes; for example, 's'. Some nonprinting and special characters require an escape sequence.

Character Constants	
`'\a'`	alert
`'\\'`	backslash
`'\b'`	backspace
`'\r'`	carriage return
`'\"'`	double quote
`'\f'`	formfeed
`'\t'`	tab
`'\n'`	newline
`'\0'`	null character
`'\''`	single quote
`'\v'`	vertical tab
`'\101'`	octal 101 in ASCII 'A'
`'\x041'`	hexadecimal ASCII 'A'
`L'oop'`	`wchar_t` constant

Floating-point constants can be specified with or without signed integer exponents.

Floating-Point Constant Examples			Comments
`3.14f`	`1.234F`		narrow `float` constants
`0.123456`	`.123456`		`double` constants
`0.12345678L`	`0.123456781`		`long double` constants
`3.`	`3.0`	`0.3E1`	all express `double` 3.0
`300e-2`	`.03e2`	`30e-1`	also 3.0

String constants are considered `static char[]` constants. A string constant is a contiguous array of characters. String constants that are separated only by white space are implicitly concatenated into a single string. A backslash character at the end of the line indicates string continuation. A backslash preceding a double quote makes the double quote part of the string. The compiler places a null character at the end of a complete string as a sentinel or termination character.

String Constant Examples	Comments
""	empty string is '\0'
"OOP 4ME"	'O' 'O' 'P' ' ' '4' 'M' 'E' '\0'
"my \"quote \" is escaped"	\" used for embedding "
"a multiline string \ is also possible"	\ at end of line indicates string continuation
"This is a single string, " "since it is only separated " "by whitespace."	implicitly concatenated

Enumerations define a collection of named constants called enumerators. The constants are a list of identifiers that are implicitly consecutive integer values starting with zero. They can be anonymous, or they can be distinct types.

Enumeration Constants	Comments
enum { off, on };	off == 0, on == 1
enum color { red, blue, white, green };	color is a type
enum { BOTTOM = 50, TOP = 100, OVER };	OVER == 101
enum grades { F = 59, D = 60, C = 70, B = 80, A = 90 };	all initialized

Enumeration constants are promoted to type int in expressions.

The keyword const is used to declare that an object's value is constant throughout its scope:

Using the const Keyword	Comments
const int N = 100;	N can't change
double w[N];	[uses constant expressions]
const int bus_stops[5] = { 23, 44, 57, 59, 83 };	element values, bus_stops[i], are constant

C++ uses a preprocessor to handle a set of directives, such as the include directive, to convert the program from its preprocessing form to pure C++ syntax. These directives are introduced by the symbol #.

The use of `const` differs from the use of `#define`, as in

```
#define  N  100
```

In the case of the `const int N` declaration, N is a nonmodifiable lvalue of type `int`. In the case of the `define` macro, N is a constant. Also, the macro replacement of N occurs as a preprocessor substitution without regard to other scope rules.

Dr. P's Prescriptions: Constants

- For type-safety and scope reasons use `const` instead of `#define`.
- Use symbolic constants instead of numeric values in code.
- Use `enum` to group related constants, making them a type.

Prescription Discussion

Named constants aid readability by describing the purpose of the constant. They avoid errors because the actual constant is located in one place where the variable is initialized, and it is therefore easy to check or change. The use of `const` declarations associates a type and scope to the constant. This allows the compiler to type check the constant when it is used.

When the integer constants in a set are related, create an `enum` type with these values as enumerators. The compiler can use the enumerated type in assuring program correctness.

The avoidance of preprocessor substitutions allows a debugger to work more effectively because most debuggers work with the C++ source and will not reference preprocessor names.

Chapter 4

Declarations and Scope Rules

Declarations associate meaning with a given identifier. The syntax of C++ declarations is highly complex because it incorporates many disparate elements that are context dependent. A declaration provides an identifier with a type, a storage class, and a scope. (See Section 9.11, "The Declaration Statement," on page 57.) A simple declaration is often a definition as well. For a simple variable, this means the object is created and possibly initialized. For a function, it means the function body—that is, the brace-enclosed statements the function executes—are written out.

```
const int n = 17;      //n is declared and defined
int sqrt(double);      //sqrt is declared not defined
void foo()             //foo is declared and defined
{
    int  i = 5;        //i is defined and initialized
    .....              //i is automatic and local to foo
}
```

Complex declarations, such as class, function, and template declarations, are described in separate sections.

The typedef mechanism can be used to create a synonym for the type it defines.

Typedefs	Comments
typedef int BOOLEAN	used prior to bool type
typedef char *c_string;	c_string pointer to char
typedef void (*ptr_f)();	pointer to void fcn()

C++ has file scope, function scope, block scope, class scope, function prototype scope, and namespace scope. File scope, also known as global scope, extends from the point of declaration in a file to the end of that file. Function prototype scope is the scope of identifiers in the function prototype argument list, and extends to the end of the declaration. Blocks nest in a conventional way, and functions cannot be declared inside other functions or blocks.

Declarations can occur almost anywhere in a block. A declaration can also be an initializer in a for statement.

In file for_scop.cpp

```
double sum = 0.0;

for (int i = 0; i < N; ++i) {    //scope of i
   a[i] = rand();
   sum += a[i];
}                                //i out of scope
```

In this case the scope is restricted to the for statement. The obsolete rule was that the scope continued throughout the remaining statements of that block.

Selection statements, such as the if or switch statement, cannot merely control a declaration. In general, jumps and selections cannot bypass an initialization. This is not true of C.

```
if (flag)
   int  j = 6;              //illegal
else
   j = 19;

if (flag) {
   int  j = 6;              //legal within block
   cout << j;
}
```

C++ has a scope resolution operator ::. When used in the form :: *variable*, it allows access to the externally named variable. Other uses of this notation are important for classes and namespaces. Class member identifiers are local to that class. The scope resolution operator can be used to resolve ambiguities. When used in the form *class-name* :: *variable*, it accesses the named variable from that class:

```
class A {
public:
   static void  foo();
};

class B {
public:
   void  foo() { A :: foo();  ····· }
};
```

A hidden external name can be accessed by using the scope resolution operator:

In file scope1.cpp

```
int  i;                //external i
void foo(int i)        //parameter i
{
   i = ::i;            //parameter i is assigned external i
   ·····
}
```

Classes can be nested. C++ rules make the inner class scoped within the outer class. This is a source of confusion, since the rules have changed and are different from C rules.

```
class list {
public:
   ·····
private:
   class list_element {    //list::list_element scope
   public:
      list_element* next;
      int           data;
   };

   list_element* head;
};
```

Enumerations declared inside a class give the enumerator's class scope, as in

```
class foo {
public:
    enum  button { off, on } flag;
};

int main()
{
    foo  c;

    c.flag = foo::off;
    .....
}
```

4.1 Namespaces

C++ traditionally had a single, global namespace. Programs written by different people can have name clashes when combined. C++ encourages multivendor library use. This motivates the addition of a namespace scope:

```
//file gotten by including <iostream>
namespace std {                      //turn vendor library into ansi
    #include <iostream.h>
}

namespace LMPinc {                   //LMP toy company software
    class puzzles { ..... };
    class toys { ..... };
    .....
}
```

In effect, encapsulated declarations are given an outermost, or qualified, name. The using declaration allows these names to be used without the namespace identifier.

```
using namespace std;
using namespace LMPinc;
toys  top;                          //LMPinc::toys
```

The namespace declaration, like the class declaration, can be used as part of a scope resolved identifier.

Namespaces can nest:

In file namespac.cpp

```
namespace LMPout {
    int   n;
    namespace LMPin {
        int   sq(){ return n * n; }       //LMPout::n
        void  pr_my_logo();
    }
    void  LMPin::pr_my_logo()
        { cout << "LMPinc" << endl; }
}
```

Namespaces can be used to provide a unique scope similar in effect to the use of static global declarations. This is done with an unnamed namespace definition:

```
namespace { int count = 0; }          //count is unique here
//count is available in the rest of the file
void  chg_cnt(int i) { count = i; }
```

The new ANSI conforming library headers will no longer use the .h suffix. Files, such as *iostream* or *complex*, will be declared with the namespace std. No doubt vendors will continue shipping old-style headers such as *iostream.h* or *complex.h* as well, so that old code can run without change.

Most C++ programs will now begin with includes of standard library headers followed by a using declaration.

```
#include <iostream>    //std::cout is fully qualified name
#include <vector>      //STL vector templates
#include <cstddef>     //Old C libraries
using namespace std;
```

Dr. P's Prescriptions: Declarations and Scope

- Separate declarations from statements with a blank line.

- Start file-level declarations in column 1.

- Declarations should be as local as possible.

- Use `typedef` to replace multitoken type declarations.

- Use namespaces; it will enhance library reuse.

Prescription Discussion

In block-structured languages it is usual to have declarations at the head of the block separated by a blank line from the subsequent executable code. File scope declarations and preprocessor commands are by convention placed starting in column 1. This allows them to be visually identified. Block scope declarations and class member declarations are indented three to five spaces to visually identify their scope. Declarations should be as local as possible. This makes it easier to connect them to where they are used, and therefore makes the code more understandable and maintainable. Localization also hides complexity. (See adjunct program *style.cpp*.)

Chapter 5

Linkage Rules

Modern systems are built around multifile inclusion, compilation, and linkage. For C++, it is necessary to understand how multifile programs are combined. Linking separate modules requires resolving external references. The key rule is that external nonstatic variables must be defined in only one place. Use of the keyword `extern`, together with an initializer, constitutes defining a variable. Using the keyword `extern` without an initializer constitutes a declaration but not a definition. If the keyword `extern` is omitted, the resulting declaration is a definition, with or without an initializer. The following example where these files would all be linked illustrates these rules:

In file prog1.cpp

```
char  c;              //definition of c
.....
```

In file prog2.cpp

```
extern char  c;       //declaration of c
.....
```

In file prog3.cpp

```
extern int  n = 5;    //definition of n
.....
```

In file prog4.cpp

```
char        c;          //illegal second definition
extern float n;         //illegal type mismatch
extern int  k;          //illegal no definition
.....
```

Constant definitions and inline definitions at file scope are local to that file; in other words, they are implicitly static. Constant definitions can be explicitly declared extern. It is usual to place such definitions in a header file to be included with any code that needs them.

A typedef declaration is local to its file. An enumeration constant declaration has linkage internal to its file. Enumerators and typedefs that are needed in a multi-file program should be placed in a header file. Enumerators defined within a class are local to that class, and access to them requires the scope resolution operator.

Typically, declarations are placed in header files and used in code files:

```
//LMPstack.h
#ifndef LMP_stack          //avoid reinclusion
#define LMP_stack
namespace LMP {
class stack { ····· };
}
#endif

//LMPstack.cpp
#include <LMPstack.h>      //include above file as source
using namespace LMP;
.....
```

▣ Linkage Program

In file my_types.h

```
#ifndef MYTYPE             //avoid multiple inclusion problem
#define MYTYPE

typedef char* c_string;    //c_string pointer to char
typedef void (*ptr_f)();   //pointer to function
```

```
void  foo(c_string s);        //function prototypes
void  title();
void  pr_onoff();

enum { OFF, ON };             //global enumerator
extern int  x;                //x defined in mainfile.c
#endif
```

In file fcns.cpp

```
#include  <iostream.h>        //to be separately compiled
#include  "my_types.h"

void foo(c_string s)
{
   cout <<"\nOutput: " << s;
}

void title()
{
   cout << "\nTEST TYPEDEFS";
}

void pr_onoff()
{
   if (x == OFF)
       cout << "\nOFF";
   else
       cout << "\nON";
}
```

In file mainfile.cpp

```
#include  <iostream.h>
#include  "my_types.h"

int  x = 0;                   //global x referred to in fcns.c
```

```
int main()
{
    c_string  f = "foo on you";
    ptr_f     pf = pr_onoff;

    foo("ENTER 0 or 1: ");
    cin >> x;
    if ( x == ON)
        pf = &title;
    pr_onoff();
    pf();
    x = !x;
    pf();
    foo(f);
}
```

℞ Dr. P's Prescriptions: Linkage

- Place external declarations in header files and code in code files.

- Remember that, conceptually, files are modules.

Prescription Discussion

Header files, such as *iostream.h* or *vector*, are routinely used by the system to provide libraries that support important elements of C++ coding (reference TG 94). They provide external variables, function prototypes, class declarations, constant declarations, inline functions, and `typedef` declarations imported by other modules by an `#include` directive. When the header files are wrapped in `namespace` declarations, the code should have an appropriate `using` declaration, such as `using namespace std;` for accessing standard library names.

Keeping related code together makes it easier to update and document as changes occur in one central location. Associated code and internal variables implementing these header files can be maintained in code files usually having suffixes .c or .cpp. Compile this code in the line-oriented environment by compiling each file as either source or object code. For example, *bcc mainfile.cpp fcns.cpp* will compile the linkage program example above using the Borland command-line compiler.

Chapter 6

Types

The fundamental types in C++ are integral and floating-point types. The char type is the shortest integral type. The long double is the longest floating-point type.

The following table lists these types from shortest to longest. Reading across the table, leftmost, topmost element is shortest, and rightmost, bottommost element is longest. (See adjunct program *lim2.cpp*.)

Fundamental Data Types		
bool		
char	signed char	unsigned char
wchar_t		
short	int	long
unsigned short	unsigned	unsigned long
float	double	long double

Two of these data types, bool and wchar_t, were recently added by the ANSI committee, and should be available on more recent commercial compilers. (See adjunct program *newtyp.cpp*.)

The type wchar_t is intended for character sets, such as the Japanese Kana alphabet, that require characters not representable by char. Literals of this type are wide character constants. This type is an integral type, and in mixed expression follows the same rules for integral promotion.

The type bool is a break with C tradition. Over the years, many schemes have been used to achieve a Boolean type, and the new bool type removes these inconsistencies in practice. It is also an integral type. It becomes the type returned by relational, logical, and equality expressions. The `bool` constants `true` and `false` are promotable to 1 and 0, respectively. Nonzero values are assignment-convertible to `true`, and zero is assignment-convertible to `false`. It is anticipated that as compiler vendors add this type, they will provide switches or options that allow the old practice of not using `bool`.

Types can be derived from the basic types. A simple derived type is the enumeration type. The derived types allow pointer types, array types, and structure types. A generic pointer type `void*` is allowed. Both anonymous unions and anonymous enumerations are allowed, and there is also a reference type. An anonymous union can have only nonstatic public data members. A file scope anonymous union has to be declared `static`. The `class` type and the `struct` type are structure types. Union, enumeration, and structure names are type names.

Types	Comments
`void*    gen_ptr;`	a generic pointer
`int      i, &ref_i = i;`	`ref_i` is an alias for i
`enum     button { off, on };`	enumeration
`button   flag;`	`button` is now a type name
`wchar_t  w = L'yz';`	new wide character type
`bool mine = false, yours = true;` `bool* p = &my_turn;`	new boolean type
`button   set[10];`	array

`class card {`
`public:`
`   suit   s;`
`   pips   p;`
`   void   pr_card();`
`private:`
`   int cd;`
`};`
	user-defined type
	
	public data member
	
	member function
	
	private data member

`suit card::* ptr_s = &card::s;`	pointer to member

There are five storage class keywords:

Storage Class	
auto	local to blocks and implicit
register	optimization advice and automatic
extern	global scope
static	within blocks, value retained
typedef	creates synonyms for types

The keyword auto can be used within blocks, but it is redundant and is normally omitted. Automatic variables are created at block entry and destroyed at block exit. The keyword register can be used within blocks and for function parameters. It advises the compiler that for optimization purposes the program wants a variable to reside in a high-speed register. The behavior of register variables is semantically equivalent to that of automatic variables.

The keyword extern can be used within blocks and at file scope. It indicates that a variable is linked in from elsewhere. The keyword static can be used within blocks and at file scope. Inside a block, it indicates that a variable's value is retained after block exit. At file scope, it indicates that declarations have internal linkage.

There are two special type specifier keywords:

```
const              //nonmodifiable
volatile           //surpresses compiler optimization
```

The keyword const is used to indicate that a variable or function parameter has a nonmodifiable value. The keyword volatile implies that an agent undetectable to the compiler can change the variable's value; therefore the compiler cannot readily perform optimizations on code accessing this variable. Variables getting values from external agents would be volatile.

```
volatile const gmt;    //expect external time signal
```

Dr. P's Prescriptions: Types

- Use const whenever possible.
- Use the most specific type when there is a choice among types.

Prescription Discussion

The use of const is highly desirable because it protects a variable from inadvertent change and documents the use of the value. Furthermore, the compiler is at liberty to optimize code connected to constants, for example storing them in read-only high-speed memory. Type-safety is an important property of C++. Compilers are able to perform type checking statically and consequently find bugs that would be difficult to discover at run time.

The narrower the type the more safety and, frequently, the more efficiency. Integer arithmetic is usually more accurate and faster than floating-point arithmetic. A char or a short takes less space than an int or a long.

Chapter 7

Conversion Rules and Casts

C++ has both explicit conversions, called *casts,* and implicit conversions. The implicit conversions can occur in expressions, and in passing in arguments and returning expressions from functions. Many conversions are implicit, which makes C++ convenient but potentially dangerous for the novice. Implicit conversions can induce run-time bugs that are hard to detect.

The general rules are straightforward.

Automatic Expression Conversion x *op* y

1. Any char, wchar_t, short, bool, or enum is promoted to an int. Integral types unrepresentable as int are promoted to unsigned.

2. If, after the first step, the expression is of mixed type, then, according to the hierarchy of types,

   ```
   int < unsigned < long < unsigned long
       < float < double < long double
   ```

   the operand of lower type is promoted to that of the higher type, and the value of the expression has that type. Note that unsigned is promoted to unsigned long, if long cannot contain all the values of unsigned.

The new type bool is an integral type, with the bool constant true promoted to one, and the bool constant false promoted to zero.

Implicit pointer conversions also occur in C++. Any pointer type can be converted to the generic pointer of type void*. However, unlike in ANSI C, a generic pointer is not assignment-compatible with an arbitrary pointer type. This means C++ requires that generic pointers be cast to an explicit type for assignment to a nongeneric pointer variable:

```
char*   mem;
void*   gen_p;

gen_p = mem;                         //C and C++
mem   = (char*)gen_p;                //C and (obsolete) C++
mem   = static_cast<char*>(gen_p);   //C++
mem   = gen_p;                       //legal C and illegal C++
```

The name of an array is a pointer to its base element. The null pointer constant can be converted to any pointer type:

```
char*  p = 0;                //p is a null pointer
int*   x = p;                //illegal need static_cast
int*   y = 0;                //legal
```

A pointer to a class can be converted to a pointer to a publicly derived base class. This also applies to references.

In addition to implicit conversions, which can occur across assignments and in mixed expressions, there are explicit conversions called casts. If i is an int, then

```
static_cast<double>(i)
```

will cast the value of i so that the expression has type double. The variable i itself remains unchanged. The static_cast is available for a conversion that is well defined, portable, and invertible. Some more examples are:

```
static_cast<char>('A' + 1.0)
x = static_cast<double>(static_cast<int>(y) + 1)
```

Casts that are representation or system-dependent use reinterpret_cast.

```
i = reinterpret_cast<int>(&x)            //system-dependent
```

These casts are undesirable and generally should be avoided.

Two other special casts exist in C++, const_cast and dynamic_cast. A useful discussion of dynamic_cast requires understanding inheritance (see Section 12.5, "Run-Time Type Identification," on page 95). The const modifier means a variable's value is nonmodifiable. Very occasionally it is convenient to remove this restriction. This is known as casting away constness. This is done with the const_cast as in:

```
foo(const_cast<int>(c_var));     // used to invoke foo
```

Older C++ systems allow unrestricted forms of cast with the following forms:

   (*type*) *expression*   or   *type*(*expression*)

Some examples are:

```
y = i/double(7);                 //would do division in double
ptr = (char*)(i + 88);           //int to pointer value
```

These older forms are considered obsolete and will not be used in this text, but many older compilers and older source code still use them. The older casts do not differentiate among relatively safe casts, such as static_cast, and system-dependent unsafe casts, such as reinterpret_cast. The newer casts also are self-documenting; for example, a const_cast suggests its intent through its name.

In file stcast.cpp

```
enum  peer { king, prince, earl } a;
enum  animal { horse, frog, snake } b;
. . . . .
a = static_cast<peer>(frog);
```

These new casts are safer and can replace all existing cast expressions. Still, casting should be avoided, as turning a frog into a prince is rarely a good idea.

Casts	Comments
x = float(i);	C++ functional notation
x = (float) i;	C cast notation
x = static_cast<float>(i);	ANSI C++
static_cast<char>('A' + 1.0)	ANSI C++
i = reinterpret_cast<int>(&x)	ANSI C++ system-dependent
foo(const_cast<int>(c_var));	used to invoke foo() while casting away constness

A constructor of one argument is a de facto type conversion from the argument's type to the constructor's class type unless preceded by the keyword explicit. (See Section 11.1, "Constructors and Destructors," on page 72.) Consider an example of a my_string constructor:

```
my_string::my_string(const char* p)
{
    len = strlen(p);
    s = new char[len + 1];
    assert (s != 0);
    strcpy(s, p);
}
```

This is automatically a type transfer from char* to my_string. These conversions are from an already defined type to a user-defined type. However, it is not possible for the user to add a constructor to a built-in type—for example, to int or double. In the my_string example, you may also want a conversion from my_string to char*. You can do this by defining a special conversion function inside the my_string class as follows.

```
operator char*() { return s; }        //char* s is a member
```

The general form of such a member function is:

```
operator type()   { · · · · · }
```

These conversions occur implicitly in assignment expressions and in argument and return conversions from functions. Temporaries can be created by the compiler to perform these operations. These hidden temporaries can affect execution speeds.

In systems implementing the bool type, implicit conversion to bool is required for expressions controlling the if or while statement, and for the first operand of the ternary ?: operator. The obvious conversion of zero to false and nonzero to true occurs.

Dr. P's Prescriptions: Conversions

- Avoid casts as much as possible.

- Replace ordinary casts with static_cast if possible.

- Particularly avoid reinterpret_cast.

Prescription Discussion

Casts are generally a shortcut for avoiding extra coding or an efficiency hack for avoiding extra processing. In coding, casts produce code that is hard to understand and maintain. A cast by definition changes one type into another, thus it circumvents type-safety. The safest casts involve `static_cast` conversion because as compiler-defined transformations, they are portable. The least desirable casts involve `reinterpret_cast` because they reinterpret the bits without actual recomputation. They are completely system-dependent.

Chapter 8

Expressions and Operators

C++ is an operator-rich, expression-oriented language. The operators have 17 precedence levels. Operators can also have side-effects. The following table lists their precedence and associativity.

Operator Precedence and Associativity	
Operators	**Associativity**
`::` (*global scope*) `::` (*class scope*)	left to right
`()` `[]` `->` `.` (*postfix*)`++` (*postfix*)`--` `sizeof` `typedef`	left to right
`++` (*prefix*) `--`(*prefix*) `!` `~` `&` (*address*) `+` (*unary*) `-` (*unary*) `*`(*indirection*) `delete` `new` `casts`	right to left
`.*` `->*`	left to right
`*` `/` `%`	left to right
`+` `-`	left to right
`<<` `>>`	left to right
`<` `<=` `>` `>=`	left to right
`==` `!=`	left to right
`&`	left to right
`^`	left to right

Operator Precedence and Associativity	
Operators	**Associativity**
|	left to right
&&	left to right
||	left to right
?:	right to left
= += -= *= /= %= >>= <<= &= ^= |=	right to left
, *(comma operator)*	left to right

8.1 `sizeof` Expressions

The `sizeof` operator can be applied to an expression or a parenthesized type-name. It gives the size in bytes of the type to which it is applied. Its results are system-dependent.

Declarations	
`int   a, b[10];`	
Expression	**Value on gnu C++ running on a DEC Station**
`sizeof(a)`	4
`sizeof(b)`	40 the array storage
`sizeof(b[1])`	4
`sizeof(5)`	4
`sizeof(5.5L)`	8

8.2 Autoincrement and Autodecrement Expressions

C++ provides autoincrement (++) and autodecrement (--) operators in both prefix and postfix form. The postfix form behaves differently than the prefix form by changing the affected lvalue after the rest of the expression is evaluated. (See adjunct program *auto.cpp*.)

Autoincrement and Autodecrement	Equivalent Expression
j = ++i;	i = i + 1; j = i;
j = i++;	j = i; i = i + 1;
j = --i;	i = i - 1; j = i;
j = i--;	j = i; i = i - 1;

8.3 Arithmetic Expressions

Arithmetic expressions are consistent with expected practice. The following examples are grouped by precedence, highest first:

Arithmetic Expressions	Comments
-i +w	unary minus unary plus
a * b a / b i % 5	multiply divide modulus
a + b a - b	binary addition subtraction
a = 3 / 2.0;	a is assigned 1.5
a = 3 / 2;	a is assigned 1

The modulus operator % is the remainder from the division of the first argument by the second argument. It may be used only with integer types. Arithmetic expressions depend on the conversion rules given earlier. (See Chapter 7, "Conversion Rules and Casts," on page 27.) In the table above, see how the result of the division operator / depends on its argument types.

8.4 Relational, Equality, and Logical Expressions

This discussion is based on the ANSI C++ adopting a `bool` type with constants `false` and `true`. Prior to the introduction of the `bool` type, the values zero and non-zero were thought of as *false* and *true*, and were used to effect the flow of control in various statement types. The following table contains the C++ operators that are most often used to affect flow of control.

Relational, Equality, and Logical Operators		
Relational operators	less than	<
	greater than	>
	less than or equal	<=
	greater than or equal	>=
Equality operators	equal	==
	not equal	!=
Logical operators	(unary) negation	!
	logical and	&&
	logical or	||

The negation operator ! is unary. All the other relational, equality, and logical operators are binary. They operate on expressions, and yield either `true` or `false`. Logical negation can be applied to an arbitrary expression, which is then converted to `bool`. When negation is applied to a `true` value it results in `false` and when it is applied to a `false` value it results in `true`.

In the evaluation of expressions that are the operands of && and ||, the evaluation process stops as soon as the outcome `true` or `false` is known. This is called short-circuit evaluation. For example, suppose that *expr1* and *expr2* are expressions. If *expr1* has `false` value, then in

    expr1 && *expr2*

expr2 will not be evaluated because the value of the logical expression is already determined to be `false`. Similarly, if *expr1* has `true` value, then in

    expr1 || *expr2*

expr2 will not be evaluated because the value of the logical expression is already determined to be `true`.

On systems that do not implement the `bool` type, these expressions will evaluate to one and zero, instead of `true` and `false`.

Declarations and Initialization		
`int a = -5, int b = 3, c = 0;`		
Expression	Equivalent	Value
`a + 5 && b`	`((a + 5) && b)`	`false` or 0
`!(a < b) && c`	`((!(a < b)) && c)`	`false` or 0
`1 || ( a != 7)`	`(1 || (a != 7))`	`true` or 1

Note that the last expression always short-circuits to value `true`.

8.5 Assignment Expressions

In C++, assignment occurs as part of an assignment expression. The effect is to evaluate the right side of the assignment and convert it to a value compatible with the left-side variable. Assignment conversions occur implicitly, and include narrowing conversions; simple variables are lvalues.

C++ allows multiple assignments in a single statement:

    a = b + (c = 3);   is equivalent to   c = 3; a = b + c;

C++ provides assignment operators that combine an assignment and some other operator:

    a *op*= b;   is equivalent to   a = a *op* b

Declarations and Initialization	
`int     a, i, *p = &i;` `double  w, *q = &w;`	
Assignment Expressions	**Comments**
`a = i + 1;`	assigns (`i + 1`) to a
`i = w;`	legal w value converted to `int`
`q = i;`	legal integer value promoted to `double`
`*q = *p;`	legal
`q = p;`	illegal conversion between pointer types
`q = (double*)p;`	legal
`a *= a + b;`	equivalent to `a = a * (a + b);`
`a += b;`	equivalent to `a = a + b;`

8.6 Comma Expressions

The comma operator has the lowest precedence. It is a binary operator with expressions as operands. In a comma expression of the form

> *expr1, expr2*

expr1 is evaluated first, then *expr2*. The comma expression as a whole has the value and type of its right operand. The comma operator is a control point. Therefore, each expression in the comma-separated list is evaluated completely before the next expression to its right. An example would be:

> `sum = 0, i = 1`

If `i` has been declared an `int`, then this comma expression has value 1 and type `int`. The comma operator associates from left to right.

8.7 Conditional Expressions

The conditional operator ?: is unusual in that it is a ternary operator. It takes as operands three expressions. In a construct such as

expr1 ? *expr2* : *expr3*

expr1 is evaluated first. If it is `true` , then *expr2* is evaluated and its value is the value of the conditional expression as a whole. If *expr1* is `false`, then *expr3* is evaluated and its value is the value of the conditional expression as a whole. The following example uses a conditional operator to assign the smaller of two values to the variable x:

```
x = (y < z) ? y : z;
```

The parentheses are not necessary because the conditional operator has precedence over the assignment operator. However, parentheses are good style because they clarify what is being tested for.

The type of the conditional expression

expr1 ? *expr2* : *expr3*

is determined by *expr2* and *expr3*. If they are different types, then the usual conversion rules apply. The conditional expression's type cannot depend on which of the two expressions is evaluated. The conditional operator ?: associates right to left.

8.8 Bit Manipulation Expressions

C++ provides bit manipulation operators. They operate on the machine-dependent bit representation of integral operands.

Bitwise Operators	Meaning
~	unary one's complement
<<	left shift
>>	right shift
&	and
^	exclusive or
|	or

It is customary that the shift operators be overloaded to perform I/O.

8.9 Address and Indirection Expressions

The address operator & is a unary operator that yields the address, or location, where an object is stored. The indirection operator * is a unary operator that is applied to a value of type pointer. It retrieves the value from the location being pointed at. This is also known as *dereferencing*. (See adjunct program *lval.cpp*.)

Declarations and Initialization	
`int    a = 5;`	`//declaration of a`
`int*  p = &a;`	`//p points to a`
`int&  ref_a = a;`	`//alias for a`

Expression	Value
`*p = 7;`	lvalue in effect a is assigned 7
`a = *p + 1;`	rvalue 7 added to 1 and a assigned 8

8.10 **new** and **delete** Expressions

The unary operators new and delete are available to manipulate free store, which is a system-provided memory pool for objects whose lifetime is directly managed by the programmer, creating an object by using new and destroying it by using delete.

The operator new is used in the following simple forms:

new *type-name initializer*$_{opt}$
new *type-name*[*integer expression*]

The first form allocates an object of the specified type from free store. If an initializing expression is present it performs the initialization. The second form allocates an array of objects of the specified type from free store. A default initializer must be available for these objects.

The new Operator	Comments
new int	allocates an int
new char[100]	allocates an array of 100 ints
new int(99)	allocates an int initialized to 99
new char('c')	allocates a char initialized to c
new int[n][4]	allocates an array of pointers to int

In each case there are at least two effects. First, an appropriate amount of store is allocated from free storage to contain the named type. Second, the base address of the object is returned as the value of the new expression. If new fails, either the null pointer value 0 is returned, or the exception bad_alloc or xalloc is thrown (see Chapter 19, "New Features in C++," on page 187). It is desirable to test for failure.

An initializer is a parenthesized list of arguments. For a simple type, such as an int, it would be a single expression. It cannot be used to initialize arrays, but it can be an argument list to an appropriate constructor. If the type being allocated has a constructor, the allocated object will be initialized.

The operator delete is used in the following forms:

delete *expression*
delete [ ] *expression*

In both forms the expression is typically a pointer variable used in a previous new expression. The second form is used when returning storage that was allocated as an array type. The brackets indicate that a destructor should be called for each element of the array. The operator delete returns a value of type void.

The delete Operator	Comments
delete ptr	deletes the pointer to an object
delete p[i]	deletes object p[i]
delete [] p	deletes each object of type p

The operator delete destroys an object created by new, in effect returning its allocated storage to free store for reuse. If the type being deleted has a destructor, its destructor will be called. The following example uses these constructs to dynamically allocate an array.

Allocation Using new Program

In file alloc.cpp

```
//Use of new operator to dynamically allocate array
#include  <iostream.h>
#include  <assert.h>

int main()
{
   int*  data;
   int   size;

   cout << "\nEnter array size: ";
   cin >> size;

   data = new int[size];              //return int* expression
   assert (data != 0);               //assure memory obtained
   for (int i = 0; i < size; ++i)
      cout << (data[i] = i) << '\t';
   cout << endl;
   delete []data;                    //deallocate memory
}
```

The pointer variable data is used as the base address of a dynamically allocated array whose number of elements is the value of size. The new operator is used to allocate from free store sufficient storage for an object of type `int[size]`. The operator `delete` returns to free store the storage associated with the pointer variable `data`. This can be done only with objects allocated by new. There are no guarantees on what values will appear in objects allocated from free store. The programmer is responsible for properly initializing such objects.

8.10.1 Placement Syntax and Overloading

The operator new has the general form:

$::_{opt}$ new $placement_{opt}$ type-name $initializer_{opt}$

The global operator `new()` is typically used to allocate free store. The system provides a `sizeof(type)` argument to this function implicitly. Its function prototype is:

```
void* operator new(size_t size);
```

The operator new can be overloaded at the global level by adding additional parameters and calling it using placement syntax. It can be overloaded and used to override the global versions at the class level. But when allocating an array of objects, only the default global `void* operator new(size_t size)` will be called.

The `delete` operator can also be overloaded. The global version is:

```
void operator delete(void* ptr)
```

A class-specific version can be declared as

```
void operator delete(void* ptr)
```

or as

```
void operator delete(void* ptr, size_t size)
```

but only one of these forms can be used by any one class. When deallocating an array of objects, the global version will be called. This feature provides a simple mechanism for user-defined manipulation of free store. For example:

```
#include  <stddef.h>      //size_t type defined
#include  <stdlib.h>      //malloc() and free() defined

class X {
   .....
public:
   void*  operator new(size_t size)
      { return (malloc(size)); }
   void  operator delete(void* ptr) { free(ptr); }
   X(unsigned size) { new(size); }
   ~X() { delete(this); }
   .....
};
```

In this example, the class X provides overloaded forms of new() and delete(). When a class overloads operator new(), the global operator is still accessible using the scope resolution operator ::.

The *placement* syntax provides for a comma-separated argument list that is used to select an overloaded operator new() with a matching signature. These additional arguments are often used to place the constructed object at a particular address. One form of this can be found in *new.h*.

▣ Overloaded new Program

In file ovl_new.cpp

```
//overloaded new as found in <new.h>
void* operator new(size_t size, void* ptr)
      { return ptr; }

char*  buf1 = new char[1000];  //global memory
char*  buf2 = new char[2000];  //more global memory

class sma_ob {                    //needs only a few bytes
   .....
};
```

```
int main()
{
    sma_ob *p=new(buf1) sma_ob;    //place at begin buf1[]
    sma_ob *q=new(buf2) sma_ob;    //place at begin buf2[]
    sma_ob *r=new(buf2 + sizeof(sma_ob)) sma_ob;
    . . . . .
}
```

Class new() and delete() member functions are always static.

8.10.2 Error Conditions

In the absence of implemented exception handling, new returns a zero value, indicating an allocation failure.

The standard library *new.h* has the function set_new_handler(), which installs the function to be called when new fails. Calling this with value zero means a version of new that does not throw exceptions will be used. Otherwise a bad_alloc or an xalloc exception will be thrown. The implementation of *new.h* can be system-dependent.

8.11 Other Expressions

C++ considers *function call* () and *indexing* or *subscripting* [] to be operators. They have the same precedence as the member and structure pointer operators:

```
a[j + 6]             // means  *(a + j + 6)
sqrt(z + 15.5);      // returns a double
```

The global scope resolution operator is of highest precedence. The class scope resolution operator is used with a class-name to qualify a local-to-class identifier.

```
::i                  // access global i
A::foo()             // invoke member foo() defined in A
```

The pointer to member operators are   * and ->* and their precedence is below the unary operators and above the multiplicative operator. Their use is described in Section 12.4, "Pointer to Class Member," on page 94.

Dr. P's Prescriptions: Expressions and Operators

- Use parentheses to make expressions readable.

- Use new and delete instead of malloc and free.

- If new uses [], then use delete[].

- Check that new worked.

- Avoid side-effect operators, such as ++, in complex expressions unless they are used in a known idiomatic style.

Prescription Discussion

Parentheses clarify associativity and precedence in expressions where these can be difficult to follow. They can also aid readability.

The operators new and delete access heap storage and are built in to the language. They are to be preferred to the older C library functions malloc() and free(), which do not automatically understand the C++ types they are working with. The operators new and delete invoke constructors and destructors, respectively, when appropriate.

Heap allocation that fails will result in either an allocation exception being thrown, or a return value of 0 as a pointer expression indicating failure. Assertions or catches can be used as a postcondition to test whether heap allocation succeeded. These errors are system-dependent and should be routinely tested for at run time.

Chapter 9

Statements

C++ has a large variety of statement types. It uses the semicolon as a statement terminator. Braces are used to enclose multiple statements, so as to treat them as a single unit. Statements are control points. Before a new statement is executed, the actions of the previous statements must be completed. Inside statements, the compiler has some liberty to pick which parts of subexpressions are first evaluated. For example:

```
a = f(i);           //call f() and assign to a
a += g(j);          //call g() and add to a
a = f(i) + g(j);    //compiler decides calling order
```

C++ is a block-structured language where declarations are often at the head of blocks. Unlike C, declarations are statements and can be intermixed with other statements. Structured programming principles should still be followed when writing C++ code. Namely, the goto should be avoided and care should be taken that the program flow-of-control is easy to follow.

Because C++ has many side-effect possibilities in expressions, care should be exercised in avoiding system-dependent effects. For example, the side-effect operators autoincrement and autodecrement should be used sparingly in expressions where order-of-evaluation and possible compiler optimizations can lead to system-dependencies.

In many cases, C++ statements are overly unrestrictive, and good programming discipline is required to avoid error prone constructions. For example,

```
for (double x = 0.1; !(x == y); x += 0.1)
.....
```

is problematic because machine accuracy and roundoff problems will in most cases cause a failure in the terminating condition.

The following table gives a summary of general C++ statements.

Statement	C++	Comments
empty	`;`	
expression	`i = i + k;`	assignment may use conversions
compound	`{ .....` `}`	used for function definitions and structuring; same as block
goto	`goto 11;`	avoid
if	`if (p == 0)` `    cerr << "new error";`	one-branch conditional

if-else	`if (x == y)`
	`    cout << "same\n";`
	`else`
	`    cout << "unequal\n";`
		two-branch conditional

for	`for (i = 0; i < n; ++i)` `    a[i] = b[i] + c[i];`	declarations allowed in first the component
while	`while (x != y)`	zero or more iterations

do-while	`do`
	`    y = y - 1;`
	`while (y >= 0);`
		one or more iterations

switch	`switch (s) {`
	`case 1: ++i;   break;`
	`case 2: --i;   break;`
	`.....`
	`default: ++j;`
	`};`
		use break to avoid fall-through semantics and default as a last label

break	`break;`	used in switch and iteration
continue	`continue;`	used in iterations
declaration	`int i = 7;`	in a block, file, or namespace
try block	`try { ..... }`	see Section 14.2, "Try Blocks," on page 115
labeled	`error: cerr << "ERROR";`	target of goto
return	`return x * x * x;`	try for one return per function

9.1 Expression Statements

In C++, assignment occurs as part of an assignment expression. There is no assignment statement, since it is a form of expression statement:

```
a = b + 1;      //assign (b + 1) to a
++i;            //an expression statement
a + b;          //also a statement - but seemingly useless
```

C++ allows multiple assignments in a single statement:

```
a = b = c + 3;   is equivalent to   b = c + 3; a = b;
```

9.2 The Compound Statement

A compound statement in C++ is a series of statements surrounded by braces { }. The chief use of the compound statement is to group statements into an executable unit. The body of a C++ function is always a compound statement. In C, when declarations come at the beginning of a compound statement, the statement is called a block. This rule is relaxed in C++, and declaration statements may occur throughout the statement list. Wherever it is possible to place a statement, it is also possible to place a compound statement.

9.3 The `if` and `if-else` Statements

The general form of an `if` statement is:

`if` (*condition*)
    statement

If *condition* is `true`, then *statement* is executed; otherwise *statement* is skipped. After the `if` statement has been executed, control passes to the next statement. A condition is an expression or a declaration with initialization that selects flow of control.

In file if.cpp

```
if (temperature >= 32)
    cout << "Above Freezing!\n";
cout << "Fahrenheit is " << temperature << endl;
```

Here, "Above Freezing!" is printed only when `temperature` is greater than or equal to 32. The second statement is always executed.

The if-else statement has the general form

```
if (condition)
    statement1
else
    statement2
```

If *condition* is `true`, then *statement1* is executed and *statement2* is skipped; if *condition* is `false`, then *statement1* is skipped and *statement2* is executed. After the if-else statement has been executed, control passes to the next statement.

In file if.cpp

```
if (temperature >= 32)
    cout << "Above Freezing!\n";
else if (temperature >= 212)
    cout << "Above Boiling!\n";
else
    cout << "Boy it's cold " << temperature << endl;
```

Note that an `else` statement associates with its nearest `if`; this rule prevents the ambiguity of a dangling `else`.

9.4 The while Statement

The general form of a while statement is:

```
while (condition)
    statement
```

First *condition* is evaluated. If it is `true`, then *statement* is executed and control passes back to the beginning of the while loop. The effect of this is that the body of the while loop, namely *statement*, is executed repeatedly until *condition* is false. At that point control passes to the next statement. The effect of this is that *statement* can be executed zero or more times.

An example of a while statement is the following:

In file while.cpp

```
int  i = 1, sum = 0;

while (i <= 10) {
    sum += i;
    ++i;
}                              //sum is 55 on exit
```

9.5 The for Statement

The general form of a for statement is:

for (*for-init-statement*; *condition*; *expression*)
    statement
next statement

First the *for-init-statement* is evaluated, and is used to initialize a variable in the loop. Then *condition* is evaluated. If it is true, then *statement* is executed, *expression* is evaluated, and control passes back to the beginning of the for loop again, except that evaluation of *for-init-statement* is skipped. This iteration continues until *condition* is false, at which point control passes to *next statement*.

The *for-init-statement* can be an expression statement or a simple declaration. Where it is a declaration the declared variable has the scope of the for statement. Note that this scope rule has changed from the previous rule that gave such declarations scope outside the enclosing for statement.

The for statement is iterative, and is typically used with a variable that is incremented or decremented. As an example, the following code uses a for statement to sum the integers from 1 to 10:

In file forloop.cpp

```
sum = 0;
for (i = 1; i <= 10; ++i)
    sum += i;
```

Another example shows how comma expressions can be used to initialize more than one variable.

In file forloop.cpp

```
for (factorial = n, i = n - 1; i >= 1; --i)
    factorial *= i;
```

Any or all of the expressions in a `for` statement can be missing, but the two semicolons must remain. If *for-init-statement* is missing, then no initialization step is performed as part of the `for` loop. If *expression* is missing, then no incrementation step is performed as part of the `for` loop. If *condition* is missing, then no testing step is performed as part of the `for` loop. The special rule for when *condition* is missing is that the test is always *true*. Thus the `for` loop in the code

```
for (i = 1, sum = 0 ; ; sum += i++)
    cout << sum << endl;
```

is an infinite loop.

The `for` statement is one common case where a local declaration is used to provide the loop control variable, as in:

```
for (int i = 0; i < N; ++i)
    sum += a[i];                    //sum array a[0] + ... + a[N - 1]
```

The semantics are that the `int` variable i is local to the given loop. In earlier C++ systems, it was considered declared within the surrounding block. This can be confusing, and so it is reasonable to declare all automatic program variables at the heads of blocks.

9.6 The do Statement

The general form of a do statement is:

```
do
    statement
while (condition);
next statement
```

First *statement* is executed, then *condition* is evaluated. If it is `true`, then control passes back to the beginning of the do statement and the process repeats itself. When the value of *condition* is `false`, then control passes to *next statement*. For example:

In file do.cpp

```
int i = 0, sum = 0;

do {
   sum += i;
   cin >> i;
} while (i > 0);
```

9.7 The `break` and `continue` Statements

To interrupt the normal flow of control within a loop, the programmer can use the two special statements:

```
break;      and      continue;
```

The `break` statement, in addition to its use in loops, can be used in a `switch` statement. It causes an exit from the innermost enclosing loop or `switch` statement.

The following example illustrates the use of a `break` statement. A test for a negative value is made, and if it is `true`, the `break` statement causes the `for` loop to be exited. Program control jumps to the statement immediately following the loop:

In file forloop.cpp

```
for (i = 0; i < 10; ++i) {
   cin >> x;
   if (x < 0.0) {
      cout << "All done" << endl;
      break;                        // exit loop if negative
   }
   cout << sqrt(x) << endl;
}

// break jumps to here
 .....
```

The `continue` statement causes the current iteration of a loop to stop and the next iteration of the loop to begin immediately. The following code processes all characters except digits.

In file forloop.cpp

```
for (i = 0; i < MAX; ++i) {
   cin.get(c);
   if (isdigit(c))
      continue;
   .....              // process other characters
// continue jumps to here
}
```

In this example, all characters except digits are processed. When the `continue` statement is executed, control jumps to just before the closing brace. Notice that the `continue` statement ends the current iteration, whereas a `break` statement would end the loop.

A `break` statement can occur only inside the body of a `for`, `while`, `do`, or `switch` statement. The `continue` statement can occur only inside the body of a `for`, `while`, or `do` statement.

9.8 The `switch` Statement

The `switch` statement is a multiway conditional statement generalizing the `if-else` statement. Its general form is:

```
switch (condition)
   statement
```

where *statement* is typically a compound statement containing `case` labels and optionally a `default` label. Typically, a `switch` is composed of many cases, and the condition in parentheses following the keyword `switch` determines which, if any, of the cases are executed.

The following `switch` statement counts test scores by category:

In file switch.cpp

```
switch (score) {
case 9:                         //fall through to next label
case 10:
   ++a_grades; break;
case 8:
   ++b_grades; break;
case 7:
   ++c_grades; break;
default:
   ++fails;
}
```

A case label is of the form:

case *constant integral expression*:

In a switch statement, all case labels must be unique.

If no case label is selected, then control passes to the default label, if there is one. A default label is not required. If no case label is selected and there is no default label, then the switch statement is exited.

The keywords case and default cannot occur outside a switch.

The Effect of a switch Statement

1. Evaluate the integral expression in the parentheses following switch.

2. Execute the case label that has a constant value that matches the value of the expression found in step 1; or, if no match is found, execute the default label; or, if there is no default label, terminate the switch.

3. Terminate the switch when a break statement is encountered, or by "falling off the end."

A switch cannot bypass initialization of a variable unless the entire scope of the variable is bypassed:

```
switch (k) {
case 1:
   int   very_bad = 3; break;
case 2:                         //illegal: bypasses init of very_bad
   .....
}
```

```
switch (k) {
case 1:
   {
       int  d = 3; break;
   }
case 2:                          //legal: bypasses scope of d
   .....
}
```

9.9 The goto Statement

The goto statement is an unconditional branch to an arbitrary labeled statement in the function. The goto statement is considered a harmful construct in most accounts of modern programming methodology.

A label is an identifier. By executing a goto statement of the form

goto *label*;

control is unconditionally transferred to a labeled statement, as in

In file goto.cpp

```
if (d == 0.0)
   goto error;
else
   ratio = n / d;
 .....
error:  cerr << "ERROR:  division by zero" << endl;
```

Both the goto statement and its corresponding labeled statement must be in the body of the same function.

A goto cannot bypass initialization of a variable, unless the entire scope of the variable is bypassed.

```
if (i < j)
    goto max;        //illegal: bypasses init

int  crazy = 5;

max:
    . . . . .
```

9.10 The `return` Statement

The `return` statement is used for two purposes. When it is executed, program control is immediately passed back to the calling environment. In addition, if an expression follows the keyword `return`, then the value of the expression is returned to the calling environment as well. This value must be assignment-convertible to the return type of the function definition header.

A `return` statement has one of the following two forms:

```
return;
return expression;
```

Some examples are

```
return;
return 3;
return (a + b);
```

9.11 The Declaration Statement

The declaration statement can be placed nearly anywhere in a block. This lifts the C restriction that variable declarations are placed at the head of a block before executable statements (see Chapter 4, "Declarations and Scope Rules," on page 14). A declaration statement has the form

```
type variable-name;
```

Normal block structure rules apply to a variable so declared. Some examples are:

```
for (int i = 0; i < N; ++i) {     //typical for loop
   a[i] = b[i] * c[i];
   int  k = a[i];                 //k local-possibly inefficient
   .....
}
```

C++ imposes natural restrictions on transferring into blocks passed where declarations occur. These are disallowed, as are declarations that would occur only in one branch of a conditional statement.

Dr. P's Prescriptions: Statements

- One statement to a line, except that very short statements that are conceptually related can be on the same line.

- A compound statement brace comes on the same line as its controlling condition. Its matching terminating brace is lined up under the initial letter of the keyword starting the statement. Alternatively, Algol style brace alignment may be used, where the initial brace is always on its own line.

- A function body is a compound statement and starts on its own line.

- Everything after the opening (left) brace is indented a standard number of spaces, for example three spaces as in this text. The matching closing (right) brace causes subsequent statements to be lined up under it.

- Global statements or declarations start in column 1.

- With the exception of the semicolon and unary operators, a space is added after each token for readability.

- Declarations at the head of a block are followed by a blank line.

- Parenthesize the `return` expression if it is not a simple expression.

- The return from `main()` of the integer constant 0 is considered implicit. The practice of explicitly returning 0 or not is discretionary.

- To detect errors, include a `default` in the `switch` statement even when all the expected cases have been accounted for.

- Use the `break` or `continue` rather than a `goto` when possible.

Prescription Discussion

The spacing and layout guidelines conform to standard industry practice, and are used to enhance readability. For example a uniform indentation standard makes it easier to follow flow of control.

Starting global statements and preprocessing directives in column 1 is consistent with historic practice, where in the earliest C systems preprocessor directives had to be in column 1. Also, because of indentation and rest-of-line comments, this gives the most room in neatly laying out code.

The function `main()` is an integer function with the return value being passed to the system. Zero indicates correct termination and is implicitly assumed. Historically, it was required explicitly, so contemporary practice is to have a `return 0` inside `main()`. The ANSI committee endorses the new practice of not requiring it. Either practice is acceptable, but be consistent.

In most cases, you will write short function definitions. Keeping all declarations at the head of such blocks makes it easy to see what variables the function employs. These declarations should be separated for visual clarity from executable statements that follow them.

Where expressions are complicated, parentheses can aid clarity by making grouping and precedence clear. For example, if the return expression statement is complicated, it should be parenthesized for readability. Within expressions, spaces around operators make them easier to read.

Chapter 10

Functions

Special features include the use of function prototypes, overloading, default arguments, and the effects of the keywords inline, friend, and virtual. This section restricts its discussion to basic functions, overloading, call-by-value, default arguments, and inlining. Member functions are discussed in Section 11.2, "Member Functions," on page 77. Friend functions are discussed in Section 11.3, "Friend Functions," on page 78. Virtual functions are covered in Section 12.6, "Virtual Functions," on page 96. Generic functions are discussed throughout Chapter 16, "STL."

In C++, function parameters are call-by-value unless declared as reference types.

In file stats.cpp

```cpp
//stats finds a data sets average, max and min
double stats(const double data[],      //data input
             int size,
             double& max,              //maximum element found
             double& min)              //minimum element
{
   double sum = max = min = data[0];

   for (int i = 1; i < size; ++i) {
      sum += data[i];
      if (data[i] > max)
         max = data[i];
      else if (data[i] < min)
         min = data[i];
      }
   return sum/size;
}
```

Function Declaration	C++	Comments
function	```double cube(double x)
{
return x * x * x;
}```	parameters are call-by-value; return expression must be assignment-compatible with return type
pure procedure	```void pr_int_sq(int i)
{
cout << i*i << endl;
}```	void return type denotes a pure procedure
empty argument list	```void pr_hi()
{
cout << "HI" << endl;
}```	can also be void pr_hi(void)
reference argument	```void
swap(int& i, int& j)
{
int t = i;
i = j; j = t;
}```	if invoked as swap(r, s) r and s exchange values
variable	```int
scanf(const char*,...);```	matches any number of arguments
inline	`inline cube(int x);`	inline code
default argument	```int
power(int x, int n = 2);```	power(4) yields 16 power(4, 3) yields 64
overload	```double
power(double x, int n);```	signature is double, int

10.1 Prototypes

In C++, the prototype form is

> *type name*(*argument-declaration-list*) ;

Examples are:

```
double sqrt(double x);                          //in math.h
double stats(const double data[], int size,
             double& max, double& min );
void print(const char* s);
int  printf(char* format, ...);                 //in stdio.h
```

Prototypes make C++ functions type-safe. When functions are called, the actual arguments are assignment-converted to the formal arguments type. With the above `sqrt()` prototype definition, invoking `sqrt()` guarantees that, if feasible, an argument will be converted to type `double`. When variable length argument lists are needed, the ellipsis symbol is used (...).

10.2 Call-by-Reference

Reference declarations allow C++ to have call-by-reference arguments. Let us use this mechanism to write a function, `greater()`, that exchanges two values if the first is greater than the second:

In file greater.cpp

```
//greater() using call-by-reference parameters
int greater(int& a, int& b)
{
   if (a > b) {            //exchange
      int temp = a;
      a = b;
      b = temp;
      return 1;
   }
   else
      return 0;
}
```

Now, if i and j are two `int` variables, then

```
greater(i, j)
```

will use the references to i and j to exchange, if necessary, their two values. In traditional C, this operation must be accomplished using pointers and dereferencing.

10.3 Inline Functions

The keyword `inline` suggests to the compiler that the function be converted to inline code. This keyword is used for the sake of efficiency, and generally with short functions. It is implicit for member functions that are defined within their classes. A compiler can ignore this directive for a variety of reasons, including that the function is too long. In such cases, the `inline` function is compiled as an ordinary function. An example is:

```
inline float circum(float rad) { return (pi * 2 * rad); }
```

Inline functions have internal linkage.

10.4 Default Arguments

A formal parameter can be given a default argument. However, this can be done only with contiguous formal parameters that are rightmost in the parameter list. A default value is usually an appropriate constant that occurs frequently when the function is called. The following function illustrates this point:

In file power2.cpp

```
//pow() defaults to squaring n
int pow(int n, int k = 2)                //k = 2 is default
{
    if (k == 2)
        return (n * n);
    else
        return (pow(n, k - 1) * n);
}
```

When called:

```
r_sqrd = pow(r);                         //return r*r
r_5th = pow(r, 5);                       //return r*r*r*r*r
```

10.5 Overloading

Overloading is using the same name for multiple meanings of an operator or a function. The meaning selected will depend on the types of the arguments used by the operator or function.

Consider a function that averages the values in an array of double versus one that averages the values in an array of int. Both are conveniently named avg_arr, as shown in the following program.

Overloading Program

In file avg_arr.cpp

```
double avg_arr(const int a[], int size)
{
   int   sum = 0;

   for (int i = 0; i < size; ++i)
      sum += a[i];                       //int arithmetic
   return (static_cast<double>(sum) / size);
}

double avg_arr(const double a[], int size)
{
   double   sum = 0.0;

   for (int i = 0; i < size; ++i)
      sum += a[i];                       //double arithmetic
   return (sum / size);
}
```

The function argument type list is called its *signature*. The return type is not a part of the signature, but the order of the arguments is crucial.

Consider the following overloaded declarations:

```
void   print(int i = 0);              //signature is int
void   print(int i, double x);        //int, double
void   print(double y, int i);        //double,int
```

When the `print()` function is invoked, the compiler matches the actual arguments to the various signatures and picks the best match. In general, there are three possibilities: a best match, an ambiguous match, and no match. Without a best match, the compiler issues an appropriate syntax error.

```
print('A');           //converts and matches int
print(str[]);         //no match, wrong type
print(15, 9);         //ambiguous
print(15, 9.0);       //matches int, double
print();              //matches int by default
```

There are two parts to the signature-matching algorithm. The first part determines a best match for each argument. The second part sees if there is one function that is a uniquely best match in each argument. This uniquely best match is defined as being a best match on at least one argument, and a "tied-for-best" match on all other arguments.

For a given argument, a best match is always an exact match. An exact match also includes an argument with an outermost const or volatile. Thus

```
void print(int i);
void print(const int& i);
```

is a redefinition error.

Whichever overloaded function is to be invoked, the invocation argument list must be matched to the declaration parameter list according to the function selection algorithm.

Overloaded Function Selection Algorithm

1. Use an exact match if found.

2. Try standard type promotions.

3. Try standard type conversions.

4. Try user-defined conversions.

5. Use a match to ellipsis if found.

Standard promotions are better than other standard conversions. These are conversions from `float` to `double`, and from `char`, `short`, or `enum` to `int`. Standard conversions also include pointer conversions.

An exact match is clearly best. Casts can be used to force such a match. The compiler will complain about ambiguous situations.

10.6 Type-Safe Linkage for Functions

Linkage rules for non-C++ functions can be specified using a linkage specification. Some examples are:

```
extern "C" atoi(const char* nptr);  //C linkage

extern "C" {                        //C linkage all functions
#include  <stdio.h>
}
```

This specification is at file scope, with C and C++ always supported. It is system-dependent if type-safe linkage for other languages is provided. Of a set of over-loaded functions with the same number, one at most can be declared to have other than C++ linkage. Class member functions cannot be declared with a linkage specification.

 Functions Program

In file mult.cpp

```
#include <iostream.h>
#include <complex.h>
#include <assert.h>

int mult(int n, int k = 2)
{
   assert(k > 1);
   if (k == 2)
      return (n * n);
   else
      return (mult(n, k - 1) * n);
}
```

```
double mult(double x, int k = 2)
{
    assert(k > 1);
    if (k == 2)
        return (x * x);
    else
        return (mult(x, k - 1) * x);
}

complex mult(complex w, int k = 2)
{
    assert(k > 1);
    if (k == 2)
        return (w * w);
    else
        return (mult(w, k - 1) * w);
}

int main()
{
    int i = 3;
    double d = 2.5;
    complex w(3,3.5); //3.0 + 3.5i

    cout << "\n3 squared and 3 cubed\n";
    cout << mult(i) << ", " << mult(i, 3)  << endl;
    cout << "\n2.5 squared and 2.5 to the 4th power\n";
    cout << mult(d) << ", " << mult(d, 4) << endl;
    cout << "\n3+3.5i to the 7th power\n";
    cout << mult(w, 7) << endl;
}
```

Dr. P's Prescriptions: Functions

- Functions should be short.

- Functions should do one job.

- Avoid subtle type conversions in overloading.

- Use explicit conversions to provide an exact match.

- Avoid the use of ellipsis notation.

- Use a `typedef` to simplify syntax when declaring function pointers.

- Overload only conceptually coherent function definitions.

Prescription Discussion

A large part of the art of writing code is properly writing functions. Think of functions as the paragraph element in an essay, and statements as sentences. Structured programming is a methodology that decomposes parts of a program into elements that are readily coded as functions. Keeping functions short makes them easier to test for correctness, maintain, and document. Like a paragraph in writing, they are meant to be a basic coherent unit that is easily grasped.

A function should have a readily grasped purpose as indicated by the function name, for example `print()`, which is clear as to intent. Do not obscure what a function does by giving it unrelated tasks. For example, if you want to print an array and find its maximum element, write two different functions.

In C++, there is little need for untyped functions with the ellipsis signature. Functions of appropriate type can be overloaded or generated from templates. This leads to type-safety, which the compiler can statically test for.

Overloading is frequently overused, making code difficult to follow and debug. In the extreme, by using function `foo()` with different signatures, one can produce any computation—clearly a poor practice.

Chapter 11

Classes

Classes are forms of heterogeneous aggregate types. They allow data hiding, inheritance, and member functions as a mechanism to provide user-defined types. An example is:

In file vect.cpp

```
//An implemenation of a safe array type vect

class vect {
public:
    explicit vect(int n = 10);        //default constructor
    vect(const vect& v);              //copy constructor
    vect(const int a[], int n);       //init by array
    ~vect() { delete [] p; }          //destructor
    int  ub() const;                  //upper bound
    int& operator[](int i) const;     //indexing
    vect& operator=(const vect& v);   //assignment
    friend ostream& operator<<(ostream& out, const vect& v)
private:
    int *p;                           //base pointer
    int  size;                        //number of elements
};
```

The keywords public, private, and protected indicate the access of members that follow. The default for class is private, and for struct is public. In the above example, the data members p and size are private. This makes them accessible solely to member functions of the same class.

Dr. P's Prescriptions: Class Style

- Indentation is as follows: `class`, access keywords, and closing brace all line up and are placed on separate lines. Member declarations are indented and line up.

- Access privileges are in order—`public`, `protected`, and `private`.

- Data members may be `private` or `protected`.

- Constructors come first, then a destructor, then other member functions.

- Friend functions are placed in the `public` section.

Prescription Discussion

The indentation rules are consistent with industry practice. The idea behind placing more visible members first is based on the same as newspaper articles—namely, what everyone needs to know comes first. What everyone needs to know is the public members. This is the interface available to all users of the class. The friend functions are to be considered part of that interface and therefore in the public access section as well.

11.1 Constructors and Destructors

A constructor is a member function whose name is the same as the class name. It constructs objects of the class type. This involves initialization of data members and, frequently, free store allocation using `new`. If a class has a constructor with a void argument list, or a list whose arguments all have defaults, then it can be a base type of an array declaration, where initialization is not explicit. Such a constructor is called the default constructor:

```
vect::vect() { ····· }              //default constructor

vect::vect(int i = 0) { ····· }     //default constructor
```

A destructor is a member function whose name is the class-name preceded by the tilde character ~. Its usual purpose is to destroy values of the class type. This is typically accomplished by using `delete`.

A constructor of the form

type::type(const *type*& x)

is used to copy one *type* value into another according to the following list.

Copy Constructor Use

1. A *type* variable is initialized by a *type* value.

2. A *type* value is passed as an argument in a function.

3. A *type* value is returned from a function.

This is called the copy constructor, and if not given explicitly, it is compiler-generated. The default is member-by-member initialization of value.

Classes with default constructors can have a derived array type. For example,

```
vect   a[5];
```

is a declaration that uses the empty argument constructor to create an array `a` of five objects, each of which is a size 10 `vect`.

There is a special syntax for initializing subelements of objects with constructors. Initializers for structure and class members can be specified in a comma-separated list that follows the constructor parameter list and precedes the code body. An initializer's form is:

member name (expression list)

As in

```
foo::foo(int* t):i(7), x(9.8), z(t)      //initializer list
{ // other executable follows here ····· }
```

When members are themselves classes with constructors, the expression list is matched to the appropriate constructor signature to invoke the correct overloaded constructor. It is not always possible to assign values to members in the body of the constructor. An initializer list is required when a nonstatic member is either a `const` or a reference. In the `class vect` example that follows, the constructors use an initializer for the member `vect::size`.

Constructors cannot be virtual, though destructors can be. Constructors and destructors are not inherited.

Constructors of a single parameter are automatically conversion functions. Consider the following class, whose purpose is to print nonvisible characters with their ASCII designations; for example, the code 07 (octal) is `alarm` or `bel`.

▣ Conversion Function Program

In file printabl.cpp

```
//ASCII printable characters

#include  <iostream.h>

class pr_char {
public:
    pr_char(int i = 0) : c(i % 128) { }
    void  print() const { cout << rep[c]; }
private:
    int           c;
    static const char*  rep[128];
};

const char*  pr_char::rep[128] = {"nul", "soh", "stx",
    .....
      "w", "x", "y", "z", "{", "|", "}", "~", "del"};
```

The constructor `pr_char::pr_char(int i = 0)` is both a default and conversion constructor. Notice that it uses initializer syntax and therefore has no need for an assignment statement in its body. The constructor creates an automatic conversion from integers to `pr_char`.

The automatic creation of a conversion constructor from a single-parameter constructor can be disabled by using the keyword `explicit` to preface a single-argument constructor.

Constructors and Destructors Program

In file vect_ast.cpp

```cpp
class vect {
public:
    //constructors and destructor
    explicit vect(int n = 10);   //default constructor
    vect(const vect& v);         //copy constructor
    vect(const int a[], int n);  //init by array
    ~vect() { delete [] p; }
    .....                        //more member functions
private:
    int*  p;                     //base pointer
    int   size;                  //number of elements
};

vect::vect(int n) : size(n)      //default constructor
{
    assert(n > 0);
    p = new int[size];
    assert (p != 0);             //allocation error
}

vect::vect(const vect& v) : size(v.size)
{                                //copy constructor
    p = new int[size];
    assert (p != 0);
    for (int i = 0; i < size; ++i)
        p[i] = v.p[i];
}

//constructor for initializing vect from an array
vect::vect(const int a[], int n) : size(n)
{
    assert(n > 0);
    p = new int[size];
    assert (p != 0);
    for (int i = 0; i < size; ++i)
        p[i] = a[i];
}
```

In Chapter 14, "Exceptions," we discuss how assertions or exceptions can be used to check on error conditions. Note the use of the `explicit` keyword in the default constructor to avoid the creation of a conversion constructor, since converting from `int` to `vect` does not make sense.

Dr. P's Prescriptions: Constructors and Destructors

- Classes with dynamically allocated memory should have both a copy constructor and an assignment operator explicitly defined.

- Initialization is preferable to assignment in constructors.

- Constructors have three uses: allocation, initialization, and conversion. Avoid other purposes.

- Destructors have two uses: deallocation and finalization. Avoid other purposes.

- Classes with virtual functions should provide virtual destructors.

- Classes that use heap allocation should check for failure (see Chapter 14, "Exceptions," on page 113).

- For single-argument constructors, disable unneeded conversions with the keyword `explicit`.

Prescription Discussion

Classes that use pointers as part of their implementation should provide explicit default and copy constructors. This avoids problems from inadvertent "shallow copies, " in which the pointer value is copied, but no new implementation is created. Usually such classes require a related overloaded definition of `operator=`.

Constructors are for initialization. In the debugging and prototyping phase of code development it is also useful to add code that outputs or tests behavior. Other work should not be carried out by a constructor, for this would be unexpected. For example, if in initializing an integer variable the system printed out its square root and whether it was prime, we would be properly upset.

Similarly, destructors are for finalization. They should retrieve resources connected with variables going out of scope. They are conceptually the inverse computation to a corresponding constructor.

For `const` and reference members an initializer list is required, because they cannot be given values through assignment. Even when member values can be assigned, initializers are preferable, because they can be more efficient and are notationally clear in purpose.

Unneeded conversions produced by conversion constructors are a source of obscure run-time bugs. Avoid this with `explicit`.

11.2 Member Functions

Member functions are functions declared within a class. As a consequence, they have access to `private`, `protected`, and `public` members of that class. If defined inside the class, they are treated as `inline` functions and are also treated, when necessary, as overloaded functions. In the class `vect`, the member function

```
int  ub() const { return (size - 1); }   //upper bound
```

is defined. In this example, the member function `ub` is `inline`, and has access to the `private` member `size`.

Member functions are invoked normally by use of the `.` or `->` operators, as in

```
vect   a(20), b;            //invoke appropriate constructor
vect*  ptr_v = &b;
int    uba = a.ub();                   //invoke member ub
ubb = ptr_v -> ub();                   //invoke member ub
```

Overloaded operator member functions, a special case of member functions, are discussed in section 11.5.

 Dr. P's Prescriptions: Member Functions

- Use public member functions called accessors to read `private` or `protected` data member values.

- Use `public` member functions called mutators to properly change `private` or `protected` member values.

Prescription Discussion

Part of the object-oriented recipe is data hiding where implementation is inaccessible to ordinary users of a class. The model is that implementation is given private or protected access. The class is manipulated by its public member functions. Simple access such as printing or retrieving data values is done by accessor member functions. This can be efficient if they are inlined. Also, it eliminates the casual user's ability to accidently and incorrectly change data values. Mutator member functions can be written that properly test whether data values are being correctly changed.

11.3 Friend Functions

The keyword `friend` is a function specifier. It allows a nonmember function access to the hidden members of the class of which it is a friend. A friend function must be declared inside the class declaration of which it is a friend. It is prefaced by the keyword `friend` and can appear anywhere in the class. Member functions of one class can be friend functions of another class. In this case, the member function is declared in the friend's class using the scope resolution operator to qualify its function name. If all member functions of one class are friend functions of a second class, this can be specified by writing `friend class` *class-name*.

The following declarations are typical:

```
class tweedledum {
    .....
    friend int  tweedledee::cheshire();
  };

class node {
    .....
    friend class tree;
     //tree member functions have access to node
};
```

In file complexc.cpp

```
class complex {
    .....
    friend complex operator+(complex);
  };
```

Dr. P's Prescriptions: Friends

- Use friends for binary operator overloading.

- Use friends when a special relationship exists between two classes.

- Use friends when special efficiency considerations exist.

- Overuse of friends indicates a bad class design.

Prescription Discussion

Friend declarations should be used for special situations and not merely as a way of circumventing access restrictions. They are commonly used for overloading operators. When a member function overloads a binary operator, the first argument is passed through the `this` pointer and the second argument is passed through the function's argument list. The second argument is subjected to assignment conversions. For example, `a + b` is equivalent to `a.operator+(b)` when overloaded with a member function, and to `operator+(a, b)` when overloaded with an ordinary function. In the second case both arguments are symmetrically subjected to assignment conversion. This symmetry is expected for most operators. Usually, writing these overloaded operators as nonmember functions requires the function be given access to private implementation, and therefore needs the `friend` designation.

Friend designation is also appropriate between tightly coupled classes. These classes are designed to intimately work together. An example is a container class, such as a list, and an iterator class for navigating the list.

In most situations apply the Taligent rule: "A programmer must confer with an architect before making friend declarations."

11.4 The `this` Pointer

The keyword `this` denotes an implicitly declared self-referential pointer. It can be used only in a nonstatic member function. A simple illustration of its use is:

In file clock.cpp

```
class clock {
public:
   clock(unsigned long i = 0);
   void  tick();                        //add one second
   clock  operator++() { tick(); return(*this); }
private:
   unsigned long  tot_secs, secs, mins, hours, days;
};
```

```
void clock::tick()
{
    clock  temp = clock(++tot_secs);

    secs = temp.secs;
    mins = temp.mins;
    hours = temp.hours;
    days = temp.days;
}
```

The overloaded `operator++()` member function uses the implicitly provided pointer `this` to return the newly incremented value of `clock`. The `this` keyword provides for a built-in self-referential pointer. It is as if `clock` implicitly declared the private member `clock* const this`. Early C++ systems allowed memory management for objects to be controlled by assignment to the `this` pointer. Such code is obsolete because the `this` pointer is nonmodifiable.

11.5 Operator Overloading

A special case of function overloading is operator overloading. The keyword `operator` is used to overload the operators. Just as a function, such as `print()`, can be given a variety of meanings that depend on its arguments, so can an operator, such as +, be given additional meanings. This allows infix expressions of both user types and built-in types to be written. The precedence and associativity remain fixed.

Operator overloading typically uses either member functions or friend functions, because both have privileged access. Overloading a unary operator using a member function has an empty argument list because the single operator argument is the implicit argument. For binary operators, member function operator overloading has, as its first argument, the implicitly passed class variable and, as its second argument, the lone argument list parameter. Friend functions and ordinary functions have both arguments specified in the parameter list.

We expand the `vect` class from Chapter 11, "Classes," on page 71, to have overloaded operators for addition, assignment, subscripting, and output.

In file vect_ovl.cpp

```
//Implementation of a safe array type vect
class vect {
public:
   .....
   int&  operator[](int i) const;
   vect&  operator=(const vect& v);
   friend vect  operator+(const vect&, const vect&);
   friend ostream&  operator<<(ostream& , const vect&)
private:
   int  *p;                    //base pointer
   int  size;                  //number of elements
};

//overloaded subscript operator
int& vect::operator[](int i) const
{
   if (i < 0 || i > (size - 1) )
      throw range_error(i);
   return p[i];
}

vect& vect::operator=(const vect& v)       //assignment op
{
   if (this != &v) {                       //check v = v

      int  s = (size < v.size) ? size : v.size;

      if (v.size != size)
         cerr << "copying different size arrays "
              << size << " and " << v.size << endl;
      for (int i = 0; i < s; ++i)
         p[i] = v.p[i];
   }
   return (*this);
}
```

```
//overloaded binary + operator
vect operator+(const vect& v1, const vect& v2)
{
   int    s = (v1.size < v2.size) ? v1.size : v2.size;

   vect   sum(s);
   if (v1.size != v2.size)
      cerr << "adding different size arrays "
            << v1.size << " and " << v2.size << endl;
   for (int i = 0; i < s; ++i)
      sum.p[i] = v1.p[i] + v2.p[i];
   return sum;
}

//overloaded put to operator
ostream& operator<<(ostream& out, const vect& v)
{
   for (int i = 0; i <= (v.size-1); ++i)
      out << v.p[i] << '\t';
   return (out << endl);
}
```

This class overloads the assignment and subscript operators as member functions. The overloaded operator<<() (put to) is made a friend of vect so that it may access the private members of vect. Overloaded operator<<() should always return type ostream so that multiple put to operations may be executed in a single expression. The overloaded binary plus operator is a friend so that conversion operations can be applied to both arguments. Note that the overloaded assignment operator checks for assignment to itself.

The ternary conditional operator ?:, the scope resolution operator ::, and the two member operators . and .* cannot be overloaded.

Overloaded postfix autoincrement and autodecrement can be distinguished by defining the postfix overloaded function as having a single unused integer argument, as in

```
class T {
public:
   //postfix ++ invoked as t.operator++(0);
   void  operator++(int);
   void  operator--(int);
};
```

There is no implied semantic relationship between the postfix and prefix forms.

Dr. P's Prescriptions: Operator Overloading

- A set of overloaded operators should be developed for scientific types, and not for nonstandard purposes.

- Overload the `operator=()` whenever the constructor uses new.

- Overloaded `operator=()` should check for assignment to itself. It should assign a value to each data member, and return *this.

Prescription Discussion

Personal algebras are a bad idea. They lead to writing dense and obscure code that is hard to follow and test. Where community-understood algebras exist, as in the mathematical and scientific disciplines, operator overloading should follow normal definitions and contain no surprises. One guideline is to be complete. For example, if the `operator==()` is defined, then define the corresponding `operator!=()`.

The assignment operator is especially important and is frequently a candidate for overloading. Any time the copy constructor of a class is explicitly defined, an analagous definition of `operator=()` should be coded. The default semantics of assignment are member-by-member, which is often incorrect when pointers are involved in a class implementation. When overloading assignment test that x = x works correctly.

11.6 `static` and `const` Member Functions

An ordinary member function invoked as

```
object.mem(i, j, k);
```

has an explicit argument list i, j, k, and an implicit argument list that is the members of `object`. The implicit arguments can be thought of as a list of arguments accessible through the `this` pointer. In contrast, a `static` member function cannot access any of the members using the `this` pointer. A `const` member function cannot modify its implicit arguments. The *salary* program illustrates these differences.

▪ const Member Functions Program

In file salary.cpp

```cpp
//Salary calculation using static and constant member functions

#include  <iostream.h>

class salary {
public:
    void  calc_bonus(const double perc)
        { your_bonus = b_sal * perc; }
    static void  reset_all(const int p)
        { all_bonus = p; }
    int  comp_tot() const
        { return (b_sal + your_bonus + all_bonus); }
private:
    int        b_sal;
    int        your_bonus;
    static int  all_bonus;          //declaration
};

int salary::all_bonus = 100;        //declare & define

int main()
{
    salary  w1(1000), w2(2000);

    w1.calc_bonus(0.2);
    w2.calc_bonus(0.15);
    salary::reset_all(400);         //also w1.reset_all(400);
    cout << " w1 " << w1.comp_tot() << "    w2 "
        << w2.comp_tot() << endl;
}
```

The `static` member `all_bonus` requires a file scope definition. It exists independent of any specific variables of type `salary` being declared. The `static` member can also be referred to as:

```cpp
salary::all_bonus
```

The `const` modifier comes between the end of the argument list and the front of the code body. It indicates that no data members will have their values changed, making the code more robust. In effect it means that the self-referential pointer is passed as `const salary* const this`.

A `static` member function can be invoked using the scope resolution operator or using a specific object; therefore these are equivalent:

```
salary::reset_all(400);
w1.reset_all(400);
(&w2) -> reset_all(400);
```

While it is legal to invoke a static member function or reference a static data member with the dot operator as in

```
w1.reset_all(400);
```

it obscures the fact that `reset_all()` is a static member. Scope resolution as in:

```
salary::reset_all(400);
```

is preferred because of clarity.

 ## Dr. P's Prescriptions: `static` and `const` Member Functions

- Use `const` for accessor member functions.
- Use `::` when invoking `static` member functions.

Prescription Discussion

Use `const` whenever possible, including when modifying member functions. The use of `const` allows the compiler to test additional features of your code. It is part of the static type-safety of the C++ language. It is also useful documentation and potentially an aid in optimization.

Using the class name with the scope resolution operator instead of the variable name with the dot operator makes it clear that the variable being referenced is `static`.

11.7 Mutable

The keyword mutable allows data members of class variables that have been declared const to remain modifiable. This reduces the need to cast away const-ness. This is a relatively new feature and is not implemented on all C++ compilers. It is used as follows.

In file mutable.cpp

```
//class with mutable members
class person {
public:
   person(const char*; int; unsigned long);
   void bday() { ++age; }
   . . . . .
private:
   const char*    name;
   mutable int    age;            //always modifiable
   unsigned long  soc_sec;
};


. . . . .

const person ira("ira pohl", 38, 1110111);
. . . . .
ira.bday();                        //okay, ira.age is mutable
```

11.8 Class Design

Occam's razor is a useful design principle. It states that entities should not be multiplied beyond necessity—or beyond completeness, invertibility, orthogonality, consistency, simplicity, efficiency, and expressiveness. Such ideals can be in conflict, and frequently involve trade-offs in arriving at a design.

⬜ Classes Program

In file my_str.cpp

```cpp
//An implementation of dynamically allocated strings

#include <string.h>                          //C string library
#include <iostream.h>
#include <assert.h>

class my_string {
public:
   my_string() : len(0)
      { s = new char[1];assert(s != 0); s[0] = 0; }
   explicit my_string(const int n);
   my_string(const my_string& str);     //copy constructor
   my_string(const char* p);            //conversion constructor
   ~my_string() { delete []s; }
   my_string& operator=(const my_string& str);
   my_string operator+(const my_string& str);
   friend ostream& operator<<(ostream& out,
                              const my_string& str);
   void concat(const my_string& a, const my_string& b);
private:
   char* s;
   int   len;
};

//default constructor
my_string::my_string(const int n)
{
   s = new char[n + 1];
   assert (s != 0);
   s[0] = 0;
   len = n;
}
```

```
//construct from char* type
my_string::my_string(const char* p)
{
    len = strlen(p);
    s = new char[len + 1];
    assert (s != 0);
    strcpy(s, p);
}

//construct from an existing my_string
my_string::my_string(const my_string& str)
{
    len = str.len;
    s = new char[len + 1];
    assert (s != 0);
    strcpy(s, str.s);
}

//overloaded assignment
my_string& my_string::operator=(const my_string& str)
{
    if (this != &str) {              //check for assign to self
        delete []s;                  //retrieve old string
        len = str.len;
        s = new char[len + 1];
        assert (s != 0);
        strcpy(s, str.s);
    }
    return (*this);
}

//string output always followed by newline
ostream& operator<<(ostream& out, const my_string& str)
{
    return (out << str.s << endl);
}
```

```
//concatenation is another way of doing addition
void my_string::concat(const my_string& a, const my_string& b)
{
    len = a.len + b.len;
    delete s;
    s = new char[len + 1];
    assert (s != 0);
    strcpy(s, a.s);
    strcat(s, b.s);
}

//binary operator plus returns a temp string
my_string my_string::operator+(const my_string& str)
{
    int lens = len + str.len;        //length of new my_string
    my_string temp(lens);

    strcpy (temp.s, s);
    strcat (temp.s, str.s);
    return temp;
}

int main()
{
    char*  tr = "The wheel that squeaks the loudest\n";
    my_string  a(str), b, author("Josh Billings\n");
    my_string  both, quote;

    b = "Is the one that gets the grease\n";
    both.concat(a, b);
    quote = both + author;
    cout << quote;
}
```

 Dr. P's Prescriptions: Class Design

- Class design should be orthogonal and follow the rule of Occam's razor.

- Class design should favor the user (client) over the implementor.

- Prefer reuse of existing class libraries to reinvention.

Prescription Discussion

An orthogonal class design is an attempt to build a minimal set of operations that gives a user a complete interface to the class. For example, you would not normally have two volume controls on a radio. Also, on a radio with multiple band, you are given a control to switch between bands and a separate control to position within a band. This is an orthogonal design. It would be possible to have separate controls for each band, but would proliferate the number of controls unnecessarily.

Prefer a design that favors the class user over the class implementor. The user must be sold on the class. If a user of a class needs a highly run-time efficient class that requires a complex implementation, the class implementor must meet that requirement or not see the class used.

Prefer using standard classes and readily purchased class libraries to reinventing them. The more standard the better. Standard libraries are readily understood and more easily maintained. Even the simplest customized class can cost several programmer days to develop. This expense is unjustified when a readily available library can be purchased.

Chapter 12

Inheritance

Inheritance is the mechanism of deriving a new class from an old one. The existing class can be added to or altered to create the derived class. A class can be derived from an existing class using the form:

class *class-name*: (public|protected|private)*opt base-name*
{
    member declarations
};

As usual, the keyword class can be replaced by the keyword struct, with the usual implication that members are by default public. The keywords public, private, and protected are available as access modifiers for class members. A public member is accessible throughout its scope. A private member is accessible to other member functions within its own class. A protected member is accessible to other member functions within its class and any class immediately derived from it. These access modifiers can be used within a class declaration in any order and with any frequency.

A derived class must have a constructor if its base class lacks a default constructor. Where the base class has constructors requiring arguments, the derived class explicitly invokes the base class constructor in its initializing list. The form of such a constructor is:

class-name(*arg-list*) : *base-name*$_{opt}$ (*base-class-arg-list*)
{
    . . . . .
};

The *base-class-arg-list* is used when invoking the appropriate base class constructor, and is executed before the body of the derived class constructor is executed.

A publicly derived class is a subtype of its base class. A variable of the derived class can in many ways be treated as if it were the base class type. A pointer whose type is pointer to base class can point to objects having the publicly derived class type. A reference to the derived class, when meaningful, may be implicitly converted to a reference to the public base class. It is possible to declare a reference to a base class and initialize it to an object of the publicly derived class.

In the following example, the vect class from Section 11.1, "Constructors and Destructors," on page 75, is used as the base class. The only modification to the base class is to make the private members protected. The following vect_bnd class is the derived class:

In file vect_bnd.cpp

```
class vect_bnd : public vect {
public:
    vect_bnd(int = 0, int = 9);          //default 10 array
    vect_bnd(vect_bnd& v);               //copy constructor
    vect_bnd(vect& v);                   //conversion constructor
    vect_bnd(const int a[], int ne, int lb = 0);
    int&  operator[](int) const;
    int   ub() const { return (u_bnd); }
    int   lb() const { return (l_bnd); }
    vect_bnd& operator=(const vect_bnd& v);
private:
    int  l_bnd, u_bnd;
};

//default constructor
vect_bnd::vect_bnd(int lb, int ub) :
         vect(ub - lb + 1), l_bnd(lb), u_bnd(ub) { }

//conversion constructor
vect_bnd::vect_bnd(vect& v) :
         vect(v), l_bnd(0), u_bnd(size - 1) { }

//copy constructor
vect_bnd::vect_bnd(vect_bnd& v) :
         vect(v), l_bnd(v.l_bnd), u_bnd(v.u_bnd) { }

vect_bnd::vect_bnd(const int a[], int n, int lb) :
         vect(a, n), l_bnd(lb), u_bnd(lb + n) { }
```

In this example, the constructors for the derived class invoke a constructor in the base class, with the argument list following the colon.

12.1 Multiple Inheritance

Multiple inheritance allows a class to be derived from more than one base class. The syntax of class headers is extended to allow a list of base classes and their privacy designation. An example is:

```
class shape {
   // class for shape interface
};

class tview {
   // class implementing text view
};

class tshape:public shape, private tview {
   // adapter of text view to shape view
};
```

In this example, the derived class tshape publicly inherits the shape base class, an interface, and privately inherits tview, an implementation of text view. This pattern of class design is called the adapater pattern (reference DP 95 pp. 139-150). It uses multiple inheritance to combine an interface with an implementation; this technique is also known as using a *mixin* class.

In general, the parental relationship between classes is described by the inheritance directed acyclic graph (DAG). The DAG is a graph structure whose nodes are classes and whose directed edges point from base to derived class.

In deriving an identically named member from different classes, ambiguities may arise. These derivations are allowed provided the user does not make an ambiguous reference to such a member.

With multiple inheritance, two base classes can be derived from a common ancestor. If both base classes are used in the ordinary way by their derived class, that class will have two subobjects of the common ancestor. This duplication can be eliminated by using virtual inheritance.

12.2 Constructor Invocation

The order of execution for initializing constructors in base and member constructors is as follows.

Order of Constructor Execution

  1. Base classes are initialized in declaration order.

  2. Members are initialized in declaration order.

Virtual base classes are constructed before any of their derived classes, and before any nonvirtual base classes. Their construction order depends on their DAG. It is a depth-first, left-to-right order. Destructors are invoked in the reverse order of the constructors.

12.3 Abstract Base Classes

A pure virtual function is a virtual member function whose body is normally undefined. Notationally, it is declared inside the class as follows.

    virtual *function prototype* = 0;

A class that has at least one pure virtual function is an abstract base class. Variables of an abstract base class cannot exist, but pointers of such a class can be defined and used polymorphically.

A pure virtual destructor must have a definition.

12.4 Pointer to Class Member

In C++, a pointer to class member is distinct from a pointer to class. A pointer to class member has type $T::*$, where T is the class name. C++ has two operators that act to dereference a pointer to class member. The pointer to member operators are:

    .*   and   ->*

Think of x.*ptr_mem as first dereferencing the pointer to obtain a member variable and then accessing the member for the designated x.

In file trio.cpp

```
class trio {
public:
    int a, b, c;
} x, y, *q = &y;

int trio::*p = &trio::b;

x.*p        //gets x.b
q ->*p      //gets y.b
```

12.5 Run-Time Type Identification

Run-time type identification (RTTI) provides a mechanism for safely determining the type pointed at by a base class pointer at run time. It involves dynamic_cast, an operator on a base class pointer; typeid, an operator for determining the type of an object; and type_info, a structure providing run-time information for the associated type.

The dynamic_cast operator has the form:

dynamic_cast< *type* >(*v*)

where *type* must be a pointer or reference to a class type and *v* must be a corresponding pointer value or reference value. It is used with inherited classes having virtual functions as follows.

```
class Base { ····· };
class Derived : Base { ····· };

void fcn(Derived* ptr)
{
    Base* bptr = dynamic_cast<Base*>(ptr);
}
```

In this example, the cast converts the pointer value ptr to a Base*. If the conversion is inappropriate, a value of 0 is returned or a bad_cast exception is thrown.

Dynamic casts also work with reference types. Conceptually, the derived type object has a subobject that corresponds to the base type. The conversion replaces the derived type pointer value or reference with an appropriate base type pointer value or reference.

The operator typeid() can be applied to a *type-name* or to an expression to determine the exact type of the argument. The operator returns a reference to the class type_info, which is supplied by the system and is defined in the header file *typeinfo* or *typeinfo.h*. The class type_info provides a name() member function returning a string that is the type name. It also provides overloaded equality operators. Remember to check the local implementation for the complete class interface.

In file typeid.cpp

```
Base* bptr;
.....
//print the type name of what bptr currently points at
cout << typeid(bptr).name() << endl;
.....
if (typeid(bptr) == typeid(Derived)) {
//do something appropriate for Derived
.....
}
```

Bad dynamic casts and typeid operations can be made to throw the exceptions bad_cast and bad_typeid, so the user can choose between dealing with the NULL pointer or catching an exception.

12.6 Virtual Functions

The keyword virtual is a function specifier that provides a mechanism for selecting at run time the appropriate member function from among base and derived class functions. It may be used only to modify member function declarations. A virtual function must be executable code. When invoked, its semantics are the same as those of other functions. In a derived class, it can be overridden. The selection of which function to invoke from among a group of overridden virtual functions is dynamic. The typical case is where a base class has a virtual function and derived classes have their versions of this function. A pointer to a base class type can point at either a base class object or a derived class object. The member function to be invoked is selected at run time. It corresponds to the object's type, not the pointer's type. In the absence of a derived type member, the base class virtual function is used by default.

Consider the following example.

Abstract Base Class Program

In file shape.cpp

```
//shape hierarchy and virtual area() calculation
#include <iostream.h>

const double PI = 3.14159;

class shape {                           //abstract base class
public:
   virtual double  area() const { return 0; }
   //virtual double area is default behavior
   virtual char* geta_name() = 0;    //pure virtual
protected:
   double  x, y;
};

class rectangle : public shape {
public:
   rectangle(double h, double w):height(h), width(w){}
   double  area() const { return (height * width); }
   char* geta_name() { return (" RECTANGLE "); }
private:
   double  height, width;
};

class circle : public shape {
public:
   circle(double r): radius(r) { }
   double  area() const
      { return (PI * radius * radius); }
   char* geta_name() { return (" CIRCLE "); }
private:
   double   radius;
};
```

```
int main()
{
    shape*      ptr_shape;
    rectangle   rec(4.1, 5.2);
    circle      cir(6.1);
    cout << "\nThis program uses hierarchies "
         << "for shapes\n";
    ptr_shape = &rec;
    cout << endl << ptr_shape -> geta_name();
    cout << "  area = " << ptr_shape -> area();
    ptr_shape = &cir;
    cout << endl << ptr_shape -> geta_name();
    cout << "  area = " << ptr_shape -> area();
}
```

The output from this program is:

```
This program uses hierarchies for shapes

RECTANGLE  area = 21.32
CIRCLE     area = 116.899
```

In each case, a different version of geta_name() and area() is executed. Selection depends on the object being pointed at.

One reason C++ is so complex is that it has many types of functions and many rule variations that apply to them. At this point, with inheritance and the introduction of virtual functions, we have seen most varieties of function. There are also those functions that are generated by template syntax, and catch() handlers that are function-like and are part of the exception mechanism. It is useful to summarize characteristics and rules applying to most of these by category. For example, inlined functions can be member or nonmember functions and can have or not have return types. Inlining forces local linkage.

Function Characteristics				
Function Category	Member	Virtual	Return Type	Special
constructor	yes	no	no	not inherited; default
destructor	yes	yes	no	not inherited; default
assignment	yes	yes	yes	not inherited
-> [] ()	yes	yes	yes	
operator	maybe	yes	yes	
conversion	yes	yes	no	no arguments
new	static	no	void*	
delete	static	no	void*	
inline	maybe	yes	maybe	local linkage
catch	no	no	no	one argument
friend	friend	no	yes	not inherited

Inheritance Program

In file student.cpp

```
#include <iostream.h>
#include <string.h>

enum year { fresh, soph, junior, senior, grad };
enum support { ta, ra, fellowship, other };
```

```
//base class student
class student {
public:
    student(char* nm, int id, double g, year x);
    friend ostream& operator<<(ostream& out, const student& stu);
protected:
    int     student_id;
    double  gpa;
    year    y;
    char    name[30];
};


//derived class grad_student
class grad_student : public student {
public:
    grad_student (char* nm, int id, double g,
                  year x, support t, char* d, char* th);
    friend ostream& operator <<(ostream& out,
                                const grad_student& gstu);
protected:
    support  s;
    char     dept[10];
    char     thesis[80];
};

student::student(char* nm, int id, double g, year x) :
                 student_id(id), gpa(g), y(x)
{
    strcpy(name, nm);
}


grad_student::grad_student (char* nm, int id, double g, year x,
                            support t, char* d, char* th) :
                            student(nm, id, g, x), s(t)
{
    strcpy(dept, d);
    strcpy(thesis, th);
}
```

```
//overloaded output operator
ostream& operator <<(ostream& out, const student& stu)
{
    cout << endl << stu.name << ", "
         << stu.student_id << ", "
         << stu.y << ", " << stu.gpa;
    return (out << endl);
}

ostream& operator<<(ostream& out, const grad_student& gstu)
{
    out << (student)gstu;              //base class info printed
    out << gstu.dept << ", " << gstu.s << endl << gstu.thesis;
    return (out << endl);
}

int main()
{
    student        s("Mae Pohl", 100, 3.425, fresh);
    grad_student  gs("Morris Pohl", 200, 3.2564, grad,
                     ta, "Pharmacy", "Retail Pharmacies");

    cout << s;
    cout << gs;
}
```

Dr. P's Prescriptions: Inheritance

- Use interface inheritance, called ISA inheritance.

- Usually a base class will be abstract.

- Minimize interactions between classes.

- Base class destructors are usually virtual.

- Avoid deep hierarchies.

- Avoid multiple inheritance.

Prescription Discussion

Public inheritance creates a class hierarchy in which a derived class object is a form of base class object. This is called ISA inheritance; it is also referred to as interface inheritance, as opposed to implementation inheritance. Class hierarchies should be about interface inheritance. In the classic example an abstract base class shape describes the properties and behaviors of all shape types using virtual and pure virtual member functions. The derived classes like `circle` implement the specifics. The `circle` ISA `shape`. A base class reference or pointer can be assigned a derived class object or address. Manipulation by such a reference or pointer can be polymorphic—namely, by using virtual functions the properly overridden function defined in the derived class is called dynamically.

Usually such a base class is abstract. This identifies the class as an important type to be used polymorphically. It guarantees that the compiler will insist on overridden member function definitions where concrete behavior for derived types is needed.

Base class destructors should be virtual (reference EC 92 pp. 42–48.) In most cases derived classes have different resource requirements, implying that returning resources through destructor finalization needs to be dynamic.

Overdoing complexity by using deep hierarchies or multiple inheritance leads to code that can be inefficient and difficult to maintain and modify.

Chapter 13

Templates

The keyword `template` is used to implement parameterized types. Rather than repeatedly recoding for each type, the template feature allows instantiation to generate code automatically for each type.

In file stack_p.cpp

```
template <class T>        //parameterize T
class stack {
public:
   stack();
   explicit stack(int s);
   T&  pop();
   void  push(T);
   .....
private:
   T*    item;
   int  top;
   int  size;
};

typedef stack<string> str_stack;
str_stack  s(100);        //explicit string stack variable
```

A template declaration has the form:

`template` < *template arguments* > *declaration*

and a template argument can be:

```
class identifier
argument declaration
```

The class *identifier* arguments are instantiated with a type. Other argument declarations are instantiated with constant expressions of a nonfloating type, and can be a function or address of an object with external linkage:

In file array.cpp

```
template<class T, int n >
class array_n {
   .....
private:
   T  items[n];                     //n explicitly instantiated
   .....
};


array_n<complex, 1000>  w;       //w is an array of complex
```

Member function syntax, when external to the class definition, is as follows.

```
template <class T>
T& stack<T>::pop()
{
    return(item[top--]);
}
```

The class-name used by the scope resolution operator includes the template arguments, and the member function declaration requires the template declaration as a preface to the function declaration.

13.1 Template Parameters

The above template can be rewritten with default parameters for both the int argument and the type. For example:

```
template<class T = int, int n = 100>
class array_n {
   .....
};
```

The default parameters can be instantiated when declaring variables, or can be omitted, in which case the defaults will be used.

Templates can use the keyword `typename` in place of `class`. For example:

```
template<typename T = double, double* ptr_dbl>
```

This allows the template code to use a pointer to `double` argument. Ordinary floating-point arguments are not allowed, only pointer and reference to floating-point arguments are allowed.

A template argument can also be a template parameter. For example:

```
template<typename T1, template<class T2> class T3>
```

This allows very sophisticated metatemplates—templates instantiated with templates—to be coded. Libraries such as STL can use such features.

13.2 Function Template

Until 1995 compilers allowed ordinary functions to be parameterized using a restricted form of template syntax. Only `class` *identifier* instantiation is allowed. It must occur inside the function argument list:

In file swap.cpp

```
//generic swap
template <class T>
void swap(T& x, T& y)
{
    T  temp;

    temp = x;
    x = y;
    y = temp;
}
```

```
//ANSI C++ but unavailable in many current compilers
template <class T, int n>
T foo()
{
  T  temp[n];
 .....
}

foo<char, 20>();        //use char, 20 and call foo
```

A function template is used to construct an appropriate function for any invocation that matches its arguments unambiguously:

```
swap(i, j);             //i j int - okay
swap(c1, c2);           //c1, c2 complex - okay
swap(i, ch);            //i int ch char - illegal
```

The overloading function selection algorithm is as follows.

Overloaded Function Selection Algorithm

1. Exact match with trivial conversions allowed on a nontemplate function.

2. Exact match using a function template.

3. Ordinary argument resolution on a nontemplate function.

In the previous example, an ordinary function declaration whose prototype was

```
void swap(char, char);
```

would have been invoked on swap(i, ch).

13.3 Friends

Template classes can contain friends. A friend function that does not use a template specification is universally a friend of all instantiations of the template class. A friend function that incorporates template arguments is a friend only of its instantiated class:

```
template <class T>
class matrix {
private:
    friend void  foo_bar();                 //universal
    friend vect<T>  product(vect<T> v);  //instantiated
    . . . . .
};
```

13.4 Static Members

Static members are not universal, but are specific to each instantiation:

```
template <class T>
class foo {
public:
    static int  count;
    . . . . .
};


    . . . . .
foo<int>     a, b;
foo<double>  c;
```

The static variables foo<int>::count and foo<double>::count are distinct. The variables a.count and b.count reference foo<int>::count, but c.count references foo<double>::count. It is preferable to use the form foo<*type*>::count since this makes it clear that the variable referenced is the static variable.

13.5 Specialization

When the template code is unsatisfactory for a particular argument type it can be specialized. A template function overloaded by an ordinary function of the same type—that is, one whose list of arguments and return type conform to the template declaration—is a specialization of the template. When the specialization matches the call, it is called rather than code generated from the template.

```
void maxelement<char*>(char*a[],char* &max,int size);
//specialized using strcmp() to return max string
```

This would be a specialization of the previously declared template for `template<class T>maxelement()`. Class specializations are also possible, as in:

```
class stack<foobar_obj>   { /*specialize for foobar_obj */ };
```

▢ Templates Program

In file vect_it.cpp

```
//templates for vect with associated iterator class
#include  <iostream.h>
#include  <assert.h>        //for assert
```

```
template <class T> class  vect_iterator;
template <class T>
class vect {
public:
   //constructors and destructor
   typedef T* iterator;
   explicit vect(int n = 10);          //default constructor
   vect(const vect& v);                //copy constructor
   vect(const T a[], int n);           //from array
   ~vect() { delete [] p; }
   iterator begin() { return p;}
   iterator end() { return p + size;}
   T&  operator[](int i) const;
   vect& operator=(const vect& v);
   friend vect operator+(const vect& v1, const vect& v2);
   friend ostream& operator<<(ostream& out, const vect<T>& v);
private:
   T*    p;                            //base pointer
   int   size;                         //number of elements
};

//default constructor
template <class T>
vect<T>::vect(int n = 10): size(n)
{
   assert(n > 0);
   p = new T[size];
   assert(p != 0);
}

//copy constructor
template<class T>
vect<T>::vect(const vect<T>& v)
{
   size = v.size;
   p = new T[size];
   assert (p != 0);
   for (int i = 0; i < size; ++i)
     p[i] = v.p[i];
}
```

```
//Initializing vect from an array
template<class T>
vect<T>::vect(const T a[], int n) : size (n)
{
    assert (n > 0) {
    p = new T[size];
    assert (p != 0);
    for (int i = 0; i < size; ++i)
       p[i] = a[i];
}

//overloaded subscript operator
template<class T>
T& vect<T>::operator[](int i) const
{
    assert (i >= 0 && i < size);
    return p[i];
}

//overloaded output operator
template<class T>
ostream& operator<<(ostream& out, const vect<T>& v)
{
    for (int i = 0; i <= (v.size-1); ++i)
       out << v.p[i] << '\t';
    return (out << endl);
}

template<class T>
vect<T>& vect<T>::operator=(const vect<T>& v)
{
    assert(V.size == size);
       for (int i = 0; i < size; ++i)
           p[i] = v.p[i];
    }
    return (*this);
}
```

```
template<class T> vect<T> operator+(const vect<T>& v1,
                                    const vect<T>& v2)
{
    int   s = (v1.size < v2.size) ?
              v1.size : v2.size;
    vect  sum(s);
    assert (v1.size == v2.size)
    for (int i = 0; i < s; ++i)
        sum.p[i] = p[i] + v.p[i];
    return sum;
}

template<class T>
void init_vect(vect<T>& v, int start, int incr)
{
    for (int i = 0; i <= v.ub(); ++i) {
        v[i] = start;
        start += incr;
    }
}

int main()
{
    vector<double> v(5);
    vector<double>::iterator p;
    int i = 0;
    for (p = v.begin() ; p != v.end(); ++p)
        *p = 1.5 + i++;
    do {
        --p;
        cout << *p << " , ";
    } while (p != v.begin());
    cout << endl;
}
```

Dr. P's Prescriptions: Templates

- Use templates for containers, such as stack or tree.

- Use template functions in preference to functions acting on void* arguments.

- Design templates by first writing a prototype as an ordinary class.

- Use templates in preference to inheritance.

Prescription Discussion

Templates are especially good for code that is repeatedly required with different types. Container class code is usefully generalized by coding with templates. A container is an object whose primary purpose is to store values. A classic example of a container is a stack. Templates allow such code to be reused over arbitrary type with type-safety that is checked at compile-time.

Before templates were used much generic code in C++ was written using void* arguments to functions. This generic pointer type can accept any specific pointer type as an argument. This code can largely be replaced with templates. The code is again compile-time type-checked. Also, template functions need not manipulate arguments indirectly with pointers.

Template code is easily developed through generalization of a specific typical case. Develop code with the specific case first; for example, develop code for a stack of integers. Only after all of this code is satisfactory and debugged should it be converted to a general template. Then retest this code over a selection of data types that might represent typical template use.

Templates and inheritance are both techniques for reusing code. When both techniques are possibilities for developing classes templates are preferred to inheritance because they are usually more efficient and lead to simpler class design. Inheritance couples classes.

Chapter 14

Exceptions

Classically, an exception is an unexpected condition that the program encounters and cannot cope with. An example is floating-point divide by zero. Usually the system aborts the running program.

C++ code is allowed to directly raise an exception in a try block by using the throw expression. The exception will be handled by invoking an appropriate handler selected from a list of handlers found in the handler's try block. A simple example of this is as follows.

In file vect_ex2.cpp

```
vect::vect(int n)
{  //fault tolerant constructor
   try {
      if (n < 1)
         throw (n);
      p = new int[n];
      if (p == 0)
         throw ("FREE STORE EXHAUSTED");
   }
   catch (int n) { ····· }      //catches an incorrect size
   catch (const char* error) { ····· }
                                //catches free store exhaustion
}
```

Note that new in this example is the traditional new returning zero for an allocation error. C++ systems using exceptions within new can throw an xalloc or bad_alloc exception upon failure. This replaces new returning zero upon failure to allocate. The older style error handling can be retained by using set_new_handler(0).

14.1 Throwing Exceptions

Syntactically, throw expressions come in two forms:

```
throw
throw expression
```

The throw expression raises an exception in a try block. The innermost try block is used to select the catch statement that processes the exception. The throw expression with no argument rethrows the current exception, and is typically used when you want a second handler called from the first handler to further process the exception.

The expression thrown is a static temporary object that persists until exception handling is exited. The expression is caught by a handler that may use this value. An uncaught expression terminates the program.

In file throw_it.cpp

```cpp
void foo()
{
   int  i;
   //will illustrate how an exception is thrown
   i = -15;
   throw i;
}

int main()
{
   try {
      foo();
   }
   catch(int n)
      { cerr << "exception caught\n " << n << endl; }
}
```

The integer value thrown by throw i persists until the handler with integer signature catch(int n) exits. This value is available for use within the handler as its argument.

An example of rethrowing an exception is:

```
catch(int n)
{
    .....
    throw;        //rethrown
}
```

Assuming the thrown expression was of integer type, the rethrown exception is the same persistent integer object that is handled by the nearest handler suitable for that type.

14.2 Try Blocks

Syntactically, a try block has the form

```
try
    compound statement
    handler list
```

The try block is the context for deciding which handlers are invoked on a raised exception. The order in which handlers are defined is important, as it determines the order in which a handler for a raised exception of matching type will be tried:

```
try {
    .....
    throw ("SOS");
    .....
    io_condition eof(argv[i]);
    throw (eof);
    .....
}

catch (const char*) { ..... }
catch (io_condition& x) { ..... }
```

Throw Expression Matches the Catch if It Is

1. An exact match.

2. A derived type of the public base class handler type.

3. A thrown object type that is convertible to a pointer type that is the catch argument.

It is an error to list handlers in an order that prevents them from being called. An example would be:

```
catch(void*)              //any char* would match
catch(char*)
catch(BaseTypeError&)     //always for DerivedTypeError
catch(DerivedTypeError&)
```

14.3 Handlers

Syntactically, a handler has the form

catch (*formal argument*)
compound statement

The catch looks like a function declaration of one argument without a return type.

In file catch.cpp

```
catch (const char* message)
{
    cerr << message << endl;
    exit(1);
}
```

An ellipses signature that matches any argument is allowed. Also, the formal argument can be an abstract declaration, meaning it can have type information without a variable name.

14.4 Exception Specification

Syntactically, an exception specification is part of a function declaration, and has the form

function header throw (*type list*)

The *type list* is the list of types that a `throw` expression within the function can have. The function definition and declaration must write out the exception specification identically.

If the list is empty the compiler may assume that no `throw` will be executed by the function, either directly or indirectly.

```
void foo() throw(int, over_flow);
void noex(int i) throw();
```

If an exception specification is left off, then the assumption is that an arbitrary exception can be thrown by such a function. Violations of these specifications are run-time errors. They are caught by the function `unexpected()`.

14.5 `terminate()` and `unexpected()`

The system-provided function `terminate()` is called when no handler has been provided to deal with an exception. The `abort()` function is called by default. It immediately terminates the program returning control to the operating system. Other action can be specified by using `set_terminate()` to provide a handler. These declarations are found in *except* or *except.h.*

The system-provided handler `unexpected()` is called when a function throws an exception that was not in its exception specification list. By default, the `terminate()` function is called. Otherwise, a `set_unexpected()` can be used to provide a handler.

14.6 Standard Library Exceptions

The standard library exceptions are derived from the base class `exception`. Two of the derived classes are `logic_error` and `runtime_error`. The logic-error types include `bad_cast`, `out_of_range`, and `bad_typeid`, which are intended to be thrown as indicated by their names. The run-time error types include `range_error`, `overflow_error`, and `bad_alloc`.

The base class defines a virtual function

```
virtual const char* exception::what() const throw();
```

This is intended to return a meaningful diagnostic message. This member function should be defined in each derived class. The empty throw specification list indicates that the function should not itself throw an exception.

 **Exceptions Program**

In file vect_ex.cpp

```
//Safe array type vect with exceptions
#include  <iostream.h>
#include  <stdlib.h>               //for abort
#include  <new.h>                  //for set_new_handler
#include  <strstream.h>            //build string for messages

class vect {
public:
   //constructors and destructor
   explicit vect(int n = 10);      //default constructor
   vect(const vect& v);            //copy constructor
   vect(const int a[], int n);     //init by array
   ~vect() { delete [] p; }
   int   ub() const { return (size - 1); }
   int&  operator[](int i) const;    //range checked
   vect& operator=(const vect& v);
   friend vect  operator+(const vect&, const vect&);
   friend ostream& operator <<(ostream& out, const vect& v);
private:
   int*  p;                        //base pointer
   int   size;                     //number of elements
};

//default constructor
vect::vect(int n) : size(n)
{  if (n < 1) {
      strstream s;
      s << "Default constructor parameter is bad: "
        << n << ends;
      throw (s.str());
   }
   p = new int[n];
}
```

```
//copy constructor
vect::vect(const vect& v) : size(v.size)
{
   p = new int[size];
   for (int i = 0; i < size; ++i)
      p[i] = v.p[i];
}

//constructor for initializing vect from an array
vect::vect(const int a[], int n) : size(n)
{
   if (n <= 0) {
      strstream s;
      s << "\nArray init parameter is bad: "
        << n << ends;
      throw (s.str());              //give size error
   }
   p = new int[size];
   for (int i = 0; i < size; ++i)
      p[i] = a[i];
}

//overloaded subscript operator
int& vect::operator[](int i) const
{
    if (i < 0 || i > (size - 1) ) {
      strstream s;
      s << "\nBad index: vect[" <<  i << "]" << ends;
      throw (s.str());           //throw index error
   }
   return (p[i]);
}

//overloaded output operator
ostream& operator<<(ostream& out, const vect& v)
{
   for (int i = 0; i <= (v.size-1); ++i)
      out << v.p[i] << '\t';
   return (out << endl);
}
```

```
//overloaded assignment operator
vect& vect::operator=(const vect& v)
{
   if (this != &v) {                 //check for assign to self
      int  s = (size < v.size) ? size : v.size;
      if (v.size != size)
         cerr << "copying different size arrays "
              << size << " and " << v.size << endl;
      for (int i = 0; i < s; ++i)
         p[i] = v.p[i];
   }
   return (*this);
}

vect operator+(const vect& v1, const vect& v2)
{
   int  s = (v1.size < v2.size) ? v1.size : v2.size;
   vect  sum(s);
   if (v1.size != v2.size)
      cerr << "adding different size arrays "
           << v1.size << " and " << v2.size << endl;
   for (int i = 0; i < s; ++i)
      sum.p[i] = v1.p[i] + v2.p[i];
   return sum;
}

void init_vect(vect& v, int start, int incr)
{
   for (int i = 0; i <= v.ub(); ++i) {
      v[i] = start;
      start += incr;
   }
}

//simple memory error routine which aborts
void Out_Of_Memory()
{
   cerr << "\nFREE STORE EXHAUSTED\n";
   abort();
}
```

```cpp
int main()
{
    try {
        int     array[6] = { 5, 10, 15, 20, 25, 30 };
        vect    v1, v2(5);          //use default constructor
        vect    v3 (array, 5);      //init from 1st 5 elements
        vect    v4 (v3);            //use copy constructor
        set_new_handler(Out_Of_Memory);

        //  cout << v3[20];         //force index error
        //  vect    v5(-5);         //force size error
        //  vect    v6(array, -3)   //force array error

        init_vect(v1, 1, 1);
        cout << "\nvector v1 is " << v1;
        init_vect(v2, 0, 2);
        cout << "\nvector v2 is " << v2;
        cout << "\nvector v3 is " << v3;
        v4 = v1 + v3;               //force add different size arrays
        cout << "\nvector v4 is " << v4;
    }
    //catch any errors thrown with msg
    catch (const char* msg)
    {
        cerr << endl << msg << endl;
        abort();
    }
}
```

Dr. P's Prescriptions: Exceptions

- Avoid the use of exceptions as a sophisticated transfer of control.

- Avoid using exceptions for continuing computations that have undiagnosed errors.

- Use exceptions and assertions to check pre- and postconditions.

- Program by contract where exceptions guarantee the terms.

- Use exceptions to test that the system resources are exhausted, unavailable, or corrupted.

- Use exceptions to provide soft, informative termination.

- Use exceptions to restart corrected computations.

Prescription Discussion

The exception trap is to use exceptions as a patch to fix code, much in the way the `goto` was used to hack changes to poorly designed programs. Exceptions are meant to detect errors; therefore, they should mostly be used to provide informed termination and soft failure.

Programming by contract is the ability of one part of the code to rely on guarantees from another part of the code. For example, to properly merge two lists, the merge code must rely on the input lists already being ordered. This is often done with assertions. The assertion methodology can be mimicked by exceptions that abort when guarantees are not met. An example of this is a `dynamic_cast` throwing a `bad_cast` exception when it is not able to provide the indicated conversion.

Exceptions should be thrown when requested resources are unavailable. The `bad_alloc` or `xalloc` exception thrown by `new` when it fails is an example of this approach. In such cases, there may be ways to add to the system resources, allowing the program to continue.

Unless program termination is unacceptable, as in mission-critical real-time systems, ad hoc error correction and program resumption should be avoided. Such unexpected conditions should be diagnosed and the code redone. Special techniques exist for mission-critical code.

Chapter 15

Input/Output

This section describes *iostream.h* or *iostream* input/output. The stream I/O is described as a set of classes in *iostream.h*. These classes overload the put to and get from operators << and >>. Streams can be associated with files, and examples of file processing using *fstream.h* are given. A lot of file processing requires character-handling macros, which are found in *ctype.h* (reference IOS 93). These are also discussed in Section 15.7, "The Functions and Macros in ctype.h," on page 134. It is especially important with IO to check the vendor's documentation.

15.1 The Output Class `ostream`

Output is inserted into an object of type `ostream`, declared in the header file *iostream.h*. An operator << is overloaded in this class to perform output conversions from standard types. The overloaded left shift operator is called the *insertion* or *put to* operator. The operator is left associative and returns a value of type `ostream&`. The standard output `ostream` corresponding to `stdout` is `cout`, and the standard output `ostream` corresponding to `stderr` is `cerr`.

The effect of executing a simple output statement such as

```
cout << "x = " << x << '\n';
```

is to print to the screen a string of four characters, followed by an appropriate representation for the output of x, followed by a new line. The representation depends on which overloaded version of << is invoked.

The class `ostream` contains public members such as:

```
ostream& operator<<(int i);
ostream& operator<<(long i);
ostream& operator<<(double x);
ostream& operator<<(char c);
ostream& operator<<(const char* s);
ostream& put(char c);
ostream& write(const char* p, int n);
ostream& flush();
```

The member function put() outputs the character representation of c. The member function write() outputs the string of length n pointed at by p. The member function flush() forces the stream to be written. Since these are member functions, they can be used as follows.

```
cout.put('A');                       //output A

char*  str = "ABCDEFGHI";
cout.write(str + 2, 3);              //output CDE
cout.flush();                        //write buffered stream
```

15.2 Formatted Output and *iomanip.h*

The put to operator << produces by default the minimum number of characters needed to represent the output. As a consequence, output can be confusing, as seen in the following example:

In file basic_o.cpp

```
int  i = 8, j = 9;

cout << i << j ;                     //confused: prints 89
cout << i << "   " << j;             //better: prints 8   9
cout << "i= " << i << " j= " << j;   //best: i= 8 j= 9
```

Two schemes that we have used to properly space output are to have strings separating output values, and to use \n and \t to create newlines and tabbing. We can also use manipulators in the stream output to control output formatting.

A manipulator is a value or function that has a special effect on the stream it operates on. A simple example of a manipulator is endl, defined in *iostream.h*. It outputs a newline and flushes the ostream:

```
x = 1;
cout << "x = " << x << endl;
```

This immediately prints the line:

```
x = 1
```

Another manipulator, `flush`, flushes the ostream, as in:

```
cout << "x = " << x << flush;
```

This has the almost the same effect as the previous example, but does not advance to a newline.

The manipulators `dec`, `hex`, and `oct` can be used to change integer bases. The default is base 10. The conversion base remains set until explicitly changed.

I/O Manipulator Use Program

In file manip.cpp

```
//Using different bases in integer I/O
#include  <iostream.h>

int main()
{
    int   i = 10, j = 16, k = 24;
    cout << i << '\t' << j << '\t' << k << endl;
    cout << oct << i << '\t' << j << '\t' << k << endl;
    cout << hex << i << '\t' << j << '\t' << k << endl;
    cout << "Enter 3 integers, e.g. 11 11 12a" << endl;
    cin >> i >> hex >> j >> k;
    cout << dec << i << '\t' << j << '\t' << k << endl;
}
```

The resulting output is:

```
10      16      24
12      20      30
a       10      18
Enter 3 integers, e.g. 11 11 12a
11      17      298
```

The reason the final line of output is 11 followed by 17 is that the second 11 in the input was interpreted as hexadecimal, which is 16 + 1.

The above manipulators are found in *iostream.h*. Other manipulators are found in *iomanip.h*. For example, `setw(int width)` is a manipulator that changes the default field width for the next formatted I/O operation to the value of its argument. This value reverts to the default. The following table briefly lists the standard manipulators, the function of each, and where each is defined.

I/O Manipulators		
Manipulator	**Function**	**File**
endl	outputs newline and flush	*iostream.h*
ends	outputs null in string	*iostream.h*
flush	flushes the output	*iostream.h*
dec	uses decimal	*iostream.h*
hex	uses hexadecimal	*iostream.h*
oct	uses octal	*iostream.h*
ws	skips white space on input	*iostream.h*
setw(int)	sets field width	*iomanip.h*
setfill(int)	sets fill character	*iomanip.h*
setbase(int)	sets base format	*iomanip.h*
setprecision(int)	sets floating-point precision	*iomanip.h*
setiosflags(long)	sets format bits	*iomanip.h*
resetiosflags(long)	resets format bits	*iomanip.h*

15.3 User-Defined Types: Output

User-defined types have typically been printed by creating a member function
print(). Let us use the types card and deck as an example of a simple user-
defined type. We write out a set of output routines for displaying cards.

▣ User-Defined Output Program

In file pr_card.cpp

```
//card output
#include  <iostream.h>

char  pips_symbol[14] = { '?', 'A', '2', '3', '4',
       '5', '6', '7', '8', '9', 'T', 'J', 'Q', 'K' };
char  suit_symbol[4] = { 'c', 'd', 'h', 's' };

enum suit { clubs, diamonds, hearts, spades };

class pips {
public:
   void  assign(int n) { p = n % 13 + 1; }
   void  print() { cout << pips_symbol[p]; }
private:
   int  p;
};

class card {
public:
   suit  s;
   pips  p;
   void  assign(int n)
      { cd = n; s = suit(n / 13); p.assign(n); }
   void  pr_card()
      { p.print(); cout << suit_symbol[s] << " "; }
private:
   int  cd;                     //a cd is from 0 to 51
};
```

```
class deck {
public:
   void  init_deck();
   void  shuffle();
   void  deal(int, int, card*);
   void  pr_deck();
private:
   card d[52];
};

void deck::pr_deck()
{
   for (int i = 0; i < 52; ++i) {
      if (i % 13 == 0)        //13 cards to a line
         cout << endl;
      d[i].pr_card();
   }
}
```

Each card will be printed out in two characters. If d is a variable of type deck, then
d.pr_deck() will print out the entire deck, 13 cards to a line.

In keeping with the spirit of OOP, it would also be nice to overload << to accomplish the same aim. The operator << has two arguments, an ostream& and the ADT, and it must produce an ostream&. You want to use a reference to a stream and return a reference to a stream, whenever overloading << or >>, because you do not want to copy a stream object. Let us write these functions for the types card and deck:

In file pr_card2.cpp

```
ostream& operator<<(ostream& out, pips x)
{
    return (out << pips_symbol[x.p]);
}

ostream& operator<<(ostream& out, card cd)
{
   return (out << cd.p << suit_symbol[cd.s] << "  " );
}
```

```
ostream& operator<<(ostream& out, deck x)
{
    for (int i = 0; i < 52; ++i) {
        if (i % 13 == 0)        //13 cards to a line
            out << endl;
        out << x.d[i];
    }
    return out;
}
```

The functions that operate on pips and deck need to be friends of the corresponding class because they access private members.

15.4 The Input Class `istream`

An operator >> is overloaded in istream to perform input conversions to standard types. The overloaded right shift operator is called the *extraction* or *get from* operator. The standard input istream corresponding to stdin is cin.

The effect of executing a simple input statement such as

```
cin >> x >> i;
```

is to read from standard input, normally the keyboard, a value for x and then a value for i. White space is ignored.

The class istream contains public members such as

```
istream& operator>>(int& i);
istream& operator>>(long& i);
istream& operator>>(double& x);
istream& operator>>(char& c);
istream& operator>>(char* s);
istream& get(char& c);
istream& get(char* s, int n, char c = '\n');
istream& getline(char* s, int n, char c = '\n');
istream& read(char* s, int n);
```

The member function get(char& c) inputs the character representation to c, including white space characters. The member function get(char* s, int n, int c = '\n') inputs into the string pointed at by s at most n - 1 characters, up to the specified delimiter character c or an end-of-file (EOF). A terminating \0 is placed in the output string. The optionally specified default character acts as a terminator but is not placed in the output string. If not specified, the input is read up to the next newline. The member function `getline()` works like `get(char*, int, char = '\n')`, except that it discards rather than keeps the delimiter character in the designated `istream`. The member function `read(char* s, int n)` inputs into the string pointed at by `s` at most `n` characters. It sets the failbit if an end-of-file is encountered before `n` characters are read. (See Section 15.8, "Using Stream States," on page 135.) In systems that have implemented ANSI standard exceptions, the `ios_base::failure` may be thrown.

In file basic_i.cpp

```
cin.get(c);            //one character
cin.get(s, 40);        //length 40 or terminated by '\n'
cin.get(s, 10, '*');   //length 10 or terminated by *
cin.getline(s, 40);    //same as get but '\n' discarded
```

Other useful member functions:

```
int gcount();      //number of recently extracted chars
istream& ignore(int n=1, int delimeter=EOF);  //skips
int peek();        //get next character without extraction
istream& putback(char c);    //puts back character
```

When overloading the operator >> to produce input to a user-defined type, the typical form is:

```
istream& operator>>(istream& p, user-defined-type& x)
```

If the function needs access to private members of x, it must be made a friend of class x. A key point is to make x a reference parameter so that its value can be modified.

15.5 Files

C systems have stdin, stdout, and stderr as standard files. In addition, systems may define other standard files, such as stdprn and stdaux. Abstractly, a file may be thought of as a stream of characters that are processed sequentially.

Standard Files			
C	**C++**	**Name**	**Connected to**
stdin	cin	standard input file	keyboard
stdout	cout	standard output file	screen
stderr	cerr	standard error file	screen
stdprn	cprn	standard printer file	printer
stdaux	caux	standard auxiliary file	auxiliary port

The C++ stream input/output ties the first three of these standard files to cin, cout, and cerr, respectively. Typically, C++ ties cprn and caux to their corresponding standard files stdprn and stdaux. There is also clog, which is a buffered version of cerr. Other files can be opened or created by the programmer. We will show how to do this in the context of writing a program that double-spaces an existing file into an existing or new file. The file names will be specified on the command line and passed into argv.

File I/O is handled by including *fstream.h*. This contains the classes ofstream and ifstream for output and input file stream creation and manipulation. To properly open and manage an ifstream or ofstream related to a system file, you first declare it with an appropriate constructor.

```
ifstream();
ifstream(const char*, int = ios::in,
        int prot = filebuf::openprot);
ofstream();
ofstream(const char*, int = ios::out,
        int prot = filebuf::openprot);
```

The constructor of no arguments creates a variable that will later be associated with an input file. The constructor of three arguments takes as its first argument the named file. The second argument specifies the file mode. The third argument is for file protection.

The file mode arguments are defined as enumerators in class `ios` as in the follows table.

File Modes	
Argument	**Mode**
`ios::in`	input mode
`ios::app`	append mode
`ios::out`	output mode
`ios::ate`	open and seek to end of file
`ios::nocreate`	open but do not create mode
`ios::trunc`	discard contents and open
`ios::noreplace`	if file exists open fails

Thus the default for an `ifstream` is input mode, and the default for an `ofstream` is output mode. If file opening fails, the stream is put into a bad state. It can be tested with operator `!`. In libraries built with exceptions, the `failure` exception can be thrown.

Other important member functions found in *fstream.h* include:

```
//opens ifstream file
void open(const char*, int = ios::in,
        int prot = filebuf::openprot);

//opens ofstream file
void open(const char*, int = ios::out,
        int prot = filebuf::openprot);

void close();
```

These functions can be used to open and close appropriate files. If you create a file stream with the default constructor, you would normally use `open()` to associate it with a file. You could then use `close()` to close the file and open another file using the same stream. Additional member functions in other I/O classes allow for a full range of file manipulation.

15.6 Using Strings as Streams

The class strstream allows char* strings to be treated as iostreams. When using strstreams, the *strstream.h* library must be included. Newer libraries will include *sstream* that will provide istringstream and ostringstream that support in-memory IO using the standard library string type.

   The istrstream is used when input is from a string, rather than from a stream. The overloaded << get from operator may be used with istrstream variables. The forms for declaring an istrstream variable are

```
istrstream name (char* s);
istrstream name (char* s, int n);
```

where s is a string to use as input, n is the optional length of the input buffer, and *name* is used instead of cin. If n is not specified, the string must be null-terminated. The end-of-string sentinel is treated as an EOF. An example follows.

In file str_strm.cpp

```
char name[15];
int total;
char* scores[4] = { "Dave 2","Ida 5","Jim 4","Ira 8" };

istrstream ist(scores[3]); //ist uses scores[3]
ist >> name >> total;      //name: Ira , total = 8
```

The ostrstream declarations have the following forms:

```
ostrstream();
ostrstream name(char* s, int n, int mode = ios::out);
```

where s is pointer to buf to receive string, n is the optional size of buffer, and mode specifies whether the data is to be put into an empty buffer (ios::out) or appended to the existing null-terminated string in the buffer (ios::app or ios::ate). If no size is specified, the buffer is dynamically allocated. The ostrstream variable may use the overloaded put to operator << to build the string. The use of ostrstream is particularly useful when you want to construct a single string from information kept in a variety of variables. This technique is used in exception handling to build a single string variable to be used as an argument in a throw(). Our vect example, in Section 14.6, "Standard Library Exceptions," on page 118, uses this technique. In the following example, note that ost2 must contain an existing null-terminated string in order for the append to work correctly.

```
strstream ost1;
strstream ost2 (charbuf, 1000, ios::app);

ost1 << name << "   " << score << endl;
ost2 << address << city << endl << ends;
```

15.7 The Functions and Macros in *ctype.h*

The system provides a standard header file *ctype.h* or *cctype*, which contains a set of functions that are used to test characters and a set of functions that are used to convert characters. These may be implemented as macros or inline functions. This is mentioned here because of its usefulness in C++ input/output. Those functions that only test a character return an int value. The argument is type int.

ctype.h Function	Nonzero (true) Is Returned if
isalpha(c)	c is a letter
isupper(c)	c is an uppercase letter
islower(c)	c is a lowercase letter
isdigit(c)	c is a digit
isxdigit(c)	c is a hexadecimal digit
isspace(c)	c is a white space character
isalnum(c)	c is a letter or digit
ispunct(c)	c is a punctuation character
isgraph(c)	c is a printing character, except space
isprint(c)	c is a printable character
iscntrl(c)	c is a control character
isascii(c)	c is an ASCII code

Other functions provide for the appropriate conversion of a character value. Note that these functions do not change the value of c stored in memory.

ctype.h Conversion Function	Effect
toupper(c)	changes c from lowercase to uppercase
tolower(c)	changes c from uppercase to lowercase
toascii(c)	changes c to ASCII code

The ASCII code functions are usual on ASCII systems.

15.8 Using Stream States

Each stream has an associated state that can be tested. The states on existing systems are

```
enum io_state { goodbit, eofbit, failbit, badbit };
```

ANSI systems propose the type ios_base::iostate to be a bitmask type defining these values. When the nongood values are set by some IO operation, ANSI systems can throw the IO standard exception ios_base::failure. Associated with this exception is a member function what() returning a char* message that gives a reason for the failure.

The values for a particular stream can be tested using the following public member functions.

Stream State Function	What It Returns
int good()	nonzero if not EOF or other error bit set
int eof();	nonzero if istream eofbit set
int fail();	nonzero if failbit, badbit set
int bad();	nonzero if badbit set
int rdstate();	returns error state
void clear(int i = 0);	resets error state
int operator!();	return true if failbit or badbit set
operator void*	return false if failbit or badbit set

Testing for a stream being in a nongood state can protect a program from hanging up. A stream state of good means that the previous input/output operation worked and the next operation should succeed. A stream state of EOF means the previous input operation returned an end-of-file condition. A stream state of fail means the previous input/output operation failed, but the stream will be usable once the error bit is cleared. A stream state of bad means the previous input/output operation is invalid, but the stream may be usable once the error condition is corrected.

It is also possible to directly test a stream. It is nonzero if it is either in a good or EOF state:

```
if (cout << x )          //output succeeded
    . . . . .
else
    . . . . .            //output failed
```

The following program counts the number of words coming from the standard input. Normally this would be redirected to use an existing file. It illustrates ideas discussed in this and the last two sections.

Stream Program

In file word_cnt.cpp

```
//The word_cnt program for counting words
//Usage: executable < file
#include   <iostream.h>
#include   <ctype.h>
int   found_next_word();

int main()
{
   int   word_cnt = 0;

   while (found_next_word())
       ++word_cnt;
   cout << "word count is " << word_cnt << endl;
}
```

```
int found_next_word()
{
    char   c;
    int    word_sz = 0;

    cin >> c;
    while (!cin.eof() && !isspace(c)) {
        ++word_sz;
        cin.get(c);
    }
    return word_sz;
}
```

A nonwhite space character is received from the input stream and assigned to c. The while loop tests that adjacent characters are not white space. The loop terminates when either an end-of-file character or a white space character is found. The word size is returned as zero when the only nonwhite space character found is the end-of-file. One last point: The loop cannot be rewritten as

```
while (!cin.eof() && !isspace(c)) {
    ++word_sz;
    cin >> c;
}
```

because this would skip white space.

15.9 Mixing I/O Libraries

We have used *iostream.h* throughout this text. It is perfectly reasonable to want to continue using *stdio.h*. This is the standard in the C community, and it is well understood. Its disadvantage is that it is not type-safe. Functions like printf() use unchecked variable length argument lists. Stream I/O requires assignment-compatible types as arguments to its functions and overloaded operators. You might also want to mix both forms of I/O. Synchronization problems can occur because the two libraries use different buffering strategies. This can be avoided by calling:

```
ios::sync_with_stdio();
```

▣ Mixed I/O Program

In file mix_io.cpp

```cpp
//The mix_io program with syncronized IO
#include  <stdio.h>
#include  <iostream.h>

unsigned long fact(int n)
{
   unsigned long  f = 1;

   for (int i = 2; i <= n; ++i)
      f *= i;
   return f;
}

int main()
{
   int n;

   ios::sync_with_stdio();

   do {
      cout << "\nEnter n positive or 0 to halt: ";
      scanf("%d", &n);
      printf("\n fact(%d) = %ld", n, fact(n));
   } while (n > 0);
   cout << "\nend of session" << endl;
}
```

Note that for integer values greater than 12, the results will overflow. It is safe to mix stdio and iostream provided they are not mixed on the same file.

▣ I/O Program

In file dbl_sp.cpp

```cpp
//A program to double space a file
//Usage: executable  f1 f2
//f1 must be present and readable
//f2 must be writable if it exists

#include  <fstream.h>        //includes iostream.h
#include  <stdlib.h>

void double_space(ifstream& f, ofstream& t)
{
   char  c;

   while (f.get(c)) {
      t.put(c);
      if (c == '\n')
         t.put(c);
   }
}

int main(int argc, char** argv)
{
   if (argc != 3) {
      cout << "\nUsage: " << argv[0]
           << "  infile  outfile" << endl;
      exit(1);
   }

   ifstream  f_in(argv[1]);
   ofstream  f_out(argv[2]);

   if (!f_in)
      { cerr << "cannot open " << argv[1] << endl; exit(1); }
   if (!f_out) {
      { cerr << "cannot open " << argv[2] << endl; exit(1); }
   }
   double_space(f_in, f_out);
}
```

Dr. P's Prescriptions: Input/Output

- Use *iostream.h* instead of *stdio.h*.

- Provide overloaded functions for << and >> for classes.

- Remember GIGO—garbage in, garbage out.

- Output should be easily readable by a user of the program who does not have source code available.

- Input should be prompted for and checked by echoing.

Prescription Discussion

"Garbage in, garbage out" is one of the prime axioms of computation. This implies that the program must check input as rigorously as possible. One important improvement on *iostream* over *stdio* is its type-safety.

Chapter 16

STL

The standard template library (STL) is the C++ standard library providing generic programming for many standard data structures and algorithms. The library provides containers, iterators, and algorithms that support a standard for generic programming. We present a brief description emphasizing these three components.

The library is built using templates and is highly orthogonal in design. Components can be used with one another on native and user-provided types through proper instantiation of the various elements of the STL library (references STL 96 and STLP 96). Different header files are required depending on the system. Our examples conform to the ANSI standard and are encapsulated in namespace std.

 STL List Container

In file stl_cont.cpp

```
#include <iostream>
#include <list>                           //list container
#include <numeric>                        //for accumulate
using namespace std;

void print(const list<double> &lst)       //using an iterator
{                                         //to traverse lst
   list<double>::const_iterator p;
   for (p = lst.begin(); p !=lst.end(); ++p)
      cout << *p << '\t';
   cout << endl;
}
```

```
int main()
{
    double w[4] = { 0.9, 0.8, 88, -99.99 };
    list<double> z;
    for (int i = 0; i < 4; ++i)
        z.push_front(w[i]);
    print(z);
    z.sort();
    print(z);
    cout << "sum is "
        << accumulate(z.begin(), z.end(), 0.0)
        << endl;
}
```

Here, a list container is instantiated to hold doubles. An array of doubles is pushed into the list. The print() function uses an iterator to print each element of the list in turn. Notice that iterators work like pointers. They have standard interfaces that include begin() and end() member functions for starting and ending locations of the container. Also, the list interface includes a stable sorting algorithm, the sort() member function. The accumulate() function is a generic function in the numeric package that uses 0.0 as an initial value and computes the sum of the list container elements by going from the starting location to the ending location; in the above by going from z.begin() to z.end().

16.1 Containers

Containers come in two major families: sequence and associative. Sequence containers include vectors, lists, and deques; they are ordered by having a sequence of elements. Associative containers include sets, multisets, maps, and multimaps; they have keys for looking up elements. The map container is a basic associative array and requires that a comparison operation on the stored elements be defined. All varieties of container share a similar interface.

STL Typical Container Interfaces

- Constructors, including default and copy constructors

- Element access

- Element insertion

- Element deletion

- Destructor

- Iterators

Containers are traversed using iterators. These are pointer-like objects that are available as templates and optimized for use with STL containers.

In file stl_deq.cpp

```
//A typical container algorithm
double sum(const deque<double> &dq)
{
    deque<double>::const_iterator p;
    double s = 0.0;

    for (p = dq.begin(); p != dq.end(); ++p)
        s += *p ;
    return s;
}
```

The deque (double ended queue) container is traversed using a const_iterator. The iterator p is dereferenced to obtain each stored value in turn. This algorithm will work with sequence containers and with all types that have operator+=() defined.

Container classes will be designated as CAN in the following description of their interface.

STL Container Definitions	
CAN::value_type	type of value held in the CAN
CAN::reference	reference type to value
CAN::const_reference	const reference
CAN::pointer	pointer to reference type
CAN::iterator	iterator type
CAN::const_iterator	const iterator
CAN::reverse_iterator	reverse iterator
CAN::const_reverse_iterator	const reverse iterator
CAN::difference_type	represents the difference between two CAN::iterator values
CAN::size_type	size of a CAN

All container classes have these definitions available. For example, if we are using the vector container class, then vector<char>::value_type means a character value is stored in the vector container. Such a container could be traversed with a vector<char>::iterator.

Containers allow equality and comparison operators. They also have an extensive list of standard member functions.

STL Container Members	
CAN::CAN()	default constructor
CAN::CAN(c)	copy constructor
c.begin()	beginning location of CAN c
c.end()	ending location of CAN c
c.rbegin()	beginning for a reverse iterator
c.rend()	ending for a reverse iterator
c.size()	number of elements in CAN
c.max_size()	largest possible size
c.empty()	true if the CAN is empty
c.swap(d)	swap two CANs

STL Container Operators	
== != < > <= >=	equality and comparison operators using CAN::value_type

16.1.1 Sequence Containers

The sequence containers are vector, list, and deque. They have a sequence of accessible elements. In many cases the C++ array type can also be treated as a sequence container.

Sequence Container Program

In file stl_vect.cpp

```cpp
//Sequence Containers - inserting a vector into a deque

#include <iostream>
#include <deque>
#include <vector>
using namespace std;

int main()
{
    int data[5] = { 6, 8, 7, 6, 5 };
    vector<int> v(5, 6);                //5 element vector
    deque<int> d(data, data + 5);
    deque<int>::iterator p;

    cout << "\nDeque values" << endl;
    for (p = d.begin(); p != d.end(); ++p)
        cout << *p << '\t';            //print:6 8 7 6 5
    cout << endl;
    d.insert(d.begin(), v.begin(), v.end());
    for (p = d.begin(); p != d.end(); p++)
        cout << *p << '\t';            //print:6 6 6 6 6 8 7 6 5
}
```

The five-element vector v is initialized with the value 6. The deque d is initialized with values taken from the array data. The insert() member function places the v values in the specified range v.begin() to v.end() at the location d.begin().

Sequence classes will be designated as SEQ in the following description of their interface; these are in addition to the already described CAN interface.

STL Sequence Members	
SEQ::SEQ(n, v)	n elements of value v
SEQ::SEQ(b_it, e_it)	starts at b_it and go to e_it - 1
c.insert(w_it, v)	inserts v before w_it
c.insert(w_it, v, n)	inserts n copies of v before w_it
c.insert(w_it, b_it, e_it)	inserts b_it to e_it before w_it
c.erase(w_it)	erases the element at w_it
c.erase(b_it, e_it)	erases b_it to e_it

16.1.2 Associative Containers

The associative containers are set, map, multiset, and multimap. They have key-based accessible elements. These containers have an ordering relation, Compare, which is the comparison object for the associative container.

 Associative Container Program

In file stl_age.cpp

```
//Associative Containers - looking up ages
#include <iostream>
#include <map>
#include <string>
using namespace std;
```

```
int main()
{
    map<string, int, less<string> > name_age;

    name_age["Pohl,Laura"] = 7;
    name_age["Dolsberry,Betty"] = 39;
    name_age["Pohl,Tanya"] = 14;
    cout << "Laura is  " << name_age["Pohl,Laura"]
         << " years old." << endl;
}
```

In the above example, the map name_age is an associative array where the key is a string type. The Compare object is less<string>.

Associative classes will be designated as ASSOC in the following description of their interface. Keep in mind that these are in addition to the already described CAN interface.

STL Associative Definitions	
ASSOC::key_type	the retrieval key type
ASSOC::key_compare	the comparison object type
ASSOC::value_compare	the type for comparing ASSOC::value_type

The associative containers have several standard constructors for initialization.

STL Associative Constructors	
ASSOC()	default constructor using Compare
ASSOC(cmp)	constructor using cmp as the comparison object
ASSOC(b_it, e_it)	uses element range b_it to e_it using Compare
ASSOC(b_it, e_it, cmp)	uses element range b_it to e_it and cmp as the comparison object

What distinguishes associative constructors from sequence container constructors is the use of a comparison object.

STL Insert and Erase Member Functions	
`c.insert(t)`	inserts t , if no existing element has the same key as t; returns `pair <iterator, bool>` with `bool` being `true` if t was not present
`c.insert(w_it, t)`	inserts t with w_it as a starting position for the search; fails on sets and maps if key value is already present; returns position of insertion
`c.insert(b_it, e_it)`	inserts the elements in this range
`c.erase(k)`	erases elements whose key value is k, returning the number of erased elements
`c.erase(w_it)`	erases the pointed to element
`c.erase(b_it, e_it)`	erases the range of elements

The insertion works when no element of the same key is already present.

STL Member Functions	
`c.find(k)`	returns iterator to element having the given key k, otherwise ends
`c.count(k)`	returns the number of elements with k
`c.lower_bound(k)`	returns iterator to first element having value greater than or equal to k
`c.upper_bound(k)`	returns iterator to first element having value greater than k
`c.equal_range(k)`	returns an iterator pair for `lower_bound` and `upper_bound`

16.1.3 Container Adaptors

Container adaptor classes are container classes that modify existing containers to produce different public behaviors based on an existing implementation. Three provided container adaptors are stack, queue, and priority_queue.

The stack can be adapted from vector, list and deque. It needs an implementation that supports back, push_back and pop_back operations. This is a last-in, first-out data structure.

STL Adapted stack Functions	
`void push(const value_type& v)`	places v on the stack
`void pop()`	removes the top element of the stack
`value_type& top() const`	returns the top element of the stack
`bool empty() const`	returns `true` if the stack is empty
`size_type size() const`	returns the number of elements in the stack
`operator==` and `operator<`	equality and lexicographically less than

The `queue` can be adapted from `list` or `deque`. It needs an implementation that supports `empty`, `size`, `front`, `back`, `push_back` and `pop_front` operations. This is a first-in, first-out data structure.

STL Adapted queue Functions	
`void push(const value_type& v)`	places v on the end of the queue
`void pop()`	removes the front element of the queue
`value_type& front() const`	returns the front element of the queue
`value_type& back() const`	returns the back element of the queue
`bool empty() const`	returns `true` if the queue is empty
`size_type size() const`	returns the number of elements in the queue
`operator==` and `operator<`	equality and lexicographically less than

The `priority_queue` can be adapted from `vector` or `deque`. It needs an implementation that supports `empty`, `size`, `front`, `push_back`, and `pop_back` operations. A `priority_queue` also needs a comparison object for its instantiation. The top element is the largest element as defined by the comparison relationship for the `priority_queue`.

STL Adapted priority_queue Functions	
`void push(const value_type& v)`	places v in the priority_queue
`void pop()`	removes top element of the priority_queue
`value_type& top() const`	returns top element of the priority_queue
`bool empty() const`	checks for priority_queue empty
`size_type size() const`	shows number of elements in the priority_queue

We adapt the stack from an underlying vector implementation. Notice how the STL ADTs replace our individually designed implementations of these types (see Section 11.8, "Class Design," on page 87).

 Container Adaptor Program

In file stl_stak.cpp

```
//Adapt a stack from a vector
#include <iostream>
#include <stack>
#include <vector>
#include <string>
using namespace std;

int main()
{
    stack<string, vector<string> > str_stack;
    string quote[3] =
      { "The wheel that squeaks the loudest\n",
        "Is the one that gets the grease\n",
        "Josh Billings\n" };

    for (int i = 0; i < 3; ++i)
        str_stack.push(quote[i]);
    while (!str_stack.empty()) {
        cout << str_stack.top();
        str_stack.pop();
    }
}
```

16.2 Iterators

Navigation over containers is by iterator. Iterators can be thought of as an enhanced pointer type. They are templates that are instantiated as to the container class type they iterate over. There are five iterator types: input, output, forward, bidirectional, and random access (see Section 16.2.1, "Iterator Categories," on page 152). Not all iterator types may be available for a given container class. For example, random access iterators are available for vectors but not maps.

The input and output iterators have the fewest requirements. They can be used for input and output and have special implementations called istream_iterator and ostream_iterator for these purposes. (See Section 16.2.2, "Istream_iterator," on page 152, and Section 16.2.3, "Ostream_iterator," on page 153.) A forward iterator can do everything an input and output iterator can do and can additionally save a position within a container. A bidirectional iterator can go both forward and backward. A random access iterator is the most powerful and can access any element in a suitable container, such as a vector in constant time.

 Container Iterator Program

In file stl_iter.cpp

```
//Use of an output iterator
#include <iostream>
#include <set>
using namespace std;

int main()
{
    int primes[4] ={ 2, 3, 5, 7 }, *ptr = primes;
    set<int, greater<int> > s;
    set<int, greater<int> > :: const_iterator  const_s_it;

    while (ptr != primes + 4 )
       s.insert(*ptr++);
    cout << "The primes below 10 : " << endl;
    for (const_s_it = s.begin();
         const_s_it != s.end(); ++const_s_it)
       cout << *const_s_it << '\t';
}
```

The above program uses an iterator for a set container to output one-digit primes. Such an iterator needs to have the ability to autoincrement and to be dereferenced.

16.2.1 Iterator Categories

Input iterators support equality operations, dereferencing, and autoincrement. An iterator that satisfies these conditions can be used for one-pass algorithms that read values of a data structure in one direction. A special case of the input iterator is the `istream_iterator`.

Output iterators support dereferencing restricted to the left-hand side of assignment and autoincrement. An iterator that satisfies these conditions can be used for one-pass algorithms that write values to a data structure in one direction. A special case of the output iterator is the `ostream_iterator`.

Forward iterators support all input/output iterator operations and additionally support unrestricted use of assignment. This allows position within a data structure to be retained from pass to pass. Therefore, general one-directional multipass algorithms can be written with forward iterators.

Bidirectional iterators support all forward iterator operations as well as both autoincrement and autodecrement. Therefore general bidirectional multipass algorithms can be written with bidirectional iterators.

Random access iterators support all bidirectional iterator operations as well as address arithmetic operations such as indexing. In addition, random access iterators support comparison operations. Therefore, algorithms such as quicksort that require efficient random access in linear time can be written with these iterators.

Container classes and algorithms dictate the category of iterator available or needed, so `vector` containers allow random access iterators, but `lists` do not. Sorting generally requires a random access iterator, but finding requires only an input iterator.

16.2.2 `Istream_iterator`

An `istream_iterator` is derived from an `input_iterator` to work specifically with reading from streams. The template for `istream_iterator` is instantiated with a `<type, distance>`. This distance is usually specified by `ptrdiff_t`. As defined in *cstddef* or *stddef.h*, it is an integer type representing the difference between two pointer values.

In file stl_io.cpp

```
//Use of istream_iterator and ostream_iterator

#include <iterator>
#include <iostream>
#include <vector>
using namespace std;
```

```
int main()
{
    vector<int> d(5);
    int   i, sum ;
    istream_iterator<int, ptrdiff_t> in(cin);
    ostream_iterator<int> out(cout, "\t");

    cout << "enter 5 numbers" << endl;
    sum = d[0] = *in;              //input first value
    for (i = 1; i < 5; ++i) {
        d[i] = *++in;              //input consecutive values
        sum += d[i];
    }
    for (i = 0; i < 5; ++i)
        *out = d[i] ;              //output consecutive values
    cout << " sum = " << sum << endl;
}
```

The istream_iterator in is instantiated with type int and parameter ptrdiff_t. The ptrdiff_t is a distance type that the iterator uses to advance in getting the next element. In the above declaration in is constructed with the input stream cin. The first element is read and cached. The autoincrement operator advances in and reads and caches a next value of type int from the designated input stream. The ostream_iterator out is constructed with the output stream cout and the char* delimiter "\t". Thus the tab character will be issued to the stream cout after each int value is written. In this program the iterator out, when it is dereferenced, writes the assigned int value to cout.

16.2.3 Ostream_iterator

An ostream_iterator is derived from an output_iterator to work specifically with writing to streams.

In file stl_oitr.cpp

```
//Use of as ostream_iterator iterator
#include <iostream>
#include <iterator>
using namespace std;
```

```
int main()
{
   int d[5] = { 2, 3, 5, 7, 11 };                //primes
   ostream_iterator<int> out(cout, "\t");

   for (int i = 0; i < 5; ++i)
      *out = d[i] ;
}
```

The ostream_iterator can be constructed with a char* delimiter, in this case "\t". Thus the tab character will be issued to the stream cout after each int value is written. In this program the iterator out, when it is dereferenced, writes the assigned int value to cout.

16.2.4 Iterator Adaptors

Iterators can be adapted to provide backward traversal and provide traversal with insertion.

STL Iterator Adaptors

- Reverse iterators—reverse the order of iteration
- Insert iterators—insertion takes place instead of the normal overwriting mode

In the following example we use a reverse iterator to traverse a sequence.

Iterator Adaptor Program

In file stl_iadp.cpp

```
//Use of the reverse iterator

#include <iostream>
#include <vector>
using namespace std;
```

```
template <class ForwIter>
void print(ForwIter first, ForwIter last, const char* title)
{
    cout << title << endl;
    while (first != last)
        cout << *first++ << '\t';
    cout << endl;
}

int main()
{
    int     data[3] = { 9, 10, 11};
    vector<int> d(data, data + 3);
    vector<int>::reverse_iterator p = d.rbegin();

    print(d.begin(), d.end(), "Original");
    print(p, d.rend(), "Reverse");
}
```

This program uses a reverse iterator to change the direction in which the print() function prints the elements of vector d.

We will briefly list adaptors and their purpose as found in this library.

- ```
  template<class BidiIter,
      class T, class Ref = T&,
      class Distance = ptrdiff_t>
  class reverse_bidirectional_iterator;
  ```

This reverses the normal direction of iteration. Use rbegin() and rend() for range.

- ```
  template<class RandAccIter,
      class T, class Ref = T&,
      class Distance = ptrdiff_t>
  class reverse_iterator;
  ```

This reverses the normal direction of iteration. Use rbegin() and rend() for range.

- ```
  template <class Can>
    class insert_iterator;
  template <class Can, Class Iter>
  insert_iterator<Can>
    inserter(Can& c, Iter p);
  ```

  Insert iterator inserts instead of overwrites. The insertion into c is at position p.

- ```
  template <class Can>
    class front_insert_iterator;
  template <class Can>
  front_insert_iterator<Can>
    front_inserter(Can& c);
  ```

  Front insertion occurs at the front of the container and requires a push_front() member.

- ```
  template <class Can>
    class back_insert_iterator;
  template <class Can>
  back_insert_iterator<Can>
    back_inserter(Can& c);
  ```

  Back insertion occurs at the back of the container and requires a push_back() member.

16.3 Algorithms

The STL algorithms library contains the following four categories.

STL Categories of Algorithms Library

- Sorting algorithms
- Nonmutating sequence algorithms
- Mutating sequence algorithms
- Numerical algorithms

These algorithms generally use iterators to access containers instantiated on a given type. The resulting code can be competitive in efficiency with special-purpose codes.
  ```

16.3.1 Sorting algorithms

Sorting algorithms include general sorting, merges, lexicographic comparison, permutation, binary search, and selected similar operations. These algorithms have versions that use either `operator<()` or a `Compare` object. They often require random access iterators.

The following program uses the quicksort function `sort()` from STL.

▣ Sorting Algorithm Program

In file stl_sort.cpp

```cpp
#include <iostream>
#include <algorithm>
using namespace std;

const int N = 5;

int main()
{
    int    d[N], i, *e = d + N;

    for (i = 0; i < N; ++i)
        d[i] = rand();
    sort(d, e);
    for (i = 0; i < N; ++i)
        cout << d[i] << '\t';
}
```

This is a straightforward use of the library `sort` algorithm operating on the built-in array `d[]`. Notice how ordinary pointer values can be used as iterators.

We present the library prototypes for sorting algorithms.

- ```cpp
  template<class RandAcc>
  void sort(RandAcc b, RandAcc e);
  ```

This is a quicksort algorithm over the elements in the range b to e. The iterator type `RandAcc` must be a random access iterator.
  ```

- ```
  template<class RandAcc>
  void stable_sort(RandAcc b, RandAcc e);
  ```

  This is a stable sorting algorithm over the elements in the range b to e. In a stable sort equal elements remain in their relative same position.

- ```
  template<class RandAcc>
  void partial_sort(RandAcc b, RandAcc m, RandAcc e);
  ```

  This is a partial sorting algorithm over the elements in the range b to e. The range b to m is filled with elements sorted up to position m.

- ```
  template<class InputIter, class RandAcc>
  void partial_sort_copy(InputIter b, InputIter e,
                         RandAcc result_b, RandAcc result_e);
  ```

  This is a partial sorting algorithm over the elements in the range b to e. Elements sorted are taken from the input iterator range and copied to the random access iterator range. The smaller of the two ranges is used.

- ```
  template<class RandAcc>
  void nth_element(RandAcc b, RandAcc nth, RandAcc e);
  ```

  The nth element is placed in sorted order, with the rest of the elements partitioned by it. For example, if the fifth position is chosen, the four smallest elements are placed to the left of it. The remaining elements are placed to the right of it and will be greater than it.

- ```
  template<class InputIter1, class InputIter2, class OutputIter>
  OutputIter merge(InputIter1 b1, InputIter1 e1, InputIter2 b2,
                   InputIter2 e2, OutputIter result_b);
  ```

  The elements in the range b1 to e1, and b2 to e2 are merged to the starting position result_b.

- ```
  template<class BidiIter>
  void inplace_merge(BidiIter b, BidiIter m, BidiIter e);
  ```

  The elements in the range b to m and m to e are merged in place.

We will use a table to briefly list other algorithms and their purpose as found in this library.

STL Sort Related Library Functions	
`binary_search(b, e, t)`	true if t is found in b to e
`lower_bound(b, e, t)`	the first position for placing t while maintaining sorted order
`upper_bound(b, e, t)`	the last position for placing t while maintaining sorted order
`equal_range(b, e, t)`	returns an iterator pair for the range where t can be placed maintaining sorted order
`push_heap(b, e)`	places the location's e element into an already existing heap
`pop_heap(b, e)`	swaps the location's e element with the b location's element and reheaps
`sort_heap(b, e)`	performs a sort on the heap
`make_heap(b, e)`	creates a heap
`next_permutation(b, e)`	produces the next permutation
`prev_permutation(b, e)`	produces the previous permutation
`lexicographical_compare` `(b1, e1, b2, e2)`	returns **true** if sequence 1 is lexico-graphically less than sequence 2
`min(t1, t2)`	return the minimum of t1 and t2 that are call-by-reference arguments
`max(t1, t2)`	return the maximum
`min_element(b, e)`	return the position of the minimum
`max_element(b, e)`	return the position of the maximum
`includes(b1, e1, b2, e2)`	returns **true** if the second sequence is a subset of the first sequence
`set_union (b1, e1, b2,` `              e2, r)`	returns the union as an output iterator r
`set_intersection (b1, e1,` `              b2, e2, r)`	returns the set intersection as an output iterator r
`set_difference (b1, e1, b2,` `              e2, r)`	returns the set difference as an output iterator r
`set_symmetric_difference` `      (b1, e1, b2, e2, r)`	returns the set symmetric difference as an output iterator r

These algorithms have a form that uses a Compare object replacing operator<(), for example:

- ```
  template<class RandAcc, class Compare>
  void sort(RandAcc b, RandAcc e, Compare comp);
  ```

  This is a quicksort algorithm over the elements in the range b to e using comp for ordering.

16.3.2 Nonmutating Sequence Algorithms

Nonmutating algorithms do not modify the contents of the containers they work on. A typical operation is searching a container for a particular element and returning its position.

In the following program the nonmutating library function find() is used to locate the element t.

In file stl_find.cpp

```
#include <iostream>
#include <algorithm>
#include <string>
using namespace std;

int main()
{
    string words[5] = { "my", "hop", "mop", "hope", "cope"};
    string*    where;

    where = find(words, words + 5, "hop");
    cout << *++where << endl;                    //mop
    sort(words, words + 5);
    where = find(words, words + 5, "hop");
    cout << *++where << endl;                    //hope
}
```

This uses find() to look for the position of the word "hop." We print the word following "hop" before and after sorting the array words[].

We present the library prototypes for nonmutating algorithms.

- ```
  template<class InputIter, Class T>
  InputIter find(InputIter b, InputIter e, const T& t));
  ```

  This finds the position of t in the range b to e.

- ```
  template<class InputIter, Class Predicate>
  InputIter find(InputIter b, InputIter e, Predicate p));
  ```

  This finds the position of the first element that makes the predicate true in the range b to e; otherwise the position e is returned.

- ```
  template<class InputIter, Class Function>
  void for_each(InputIter b, InputIter e, Function f));
  ```

  This applies the function f to each value found in the range b to e.

We will use a table to briefly list other algorithms and their purpose as found in this library.

STL Nonmutating Sequence Library Functions	
`next_permutation(b, e)`	produces next permutation
`prev_permutation(b, e)`	produces previous permutation
`count(b, e, t, n)`	returns to n the count of elements equal to t
`count_if(b, e, p, n)`	returns to n the count of elements that make predicate p true
`adjacent_find(b, e)`	returns the first position of adjacent elements that are equal; otherwise returns e
`adjacent_find(b, e, binp)`	returns the first position of adjacent elements satisfying the binary predicate binp; otherwise returns e
`mismatch(b1, e1, b2)`	returns an iterator pair indicating the positions where elements do not match from the given sequences starting with b1 and b2
`mismatch (b1, e1, b2, binp)`	as above, with a binary predicate binp used instead of equality
`equal(b1, e1, b2)`	returns true if the indicated sequences match; otherwise returns false
`equal(b1, e1, b2, binp)`	as above, with a binary predicate binp used instead of equality
`search(b1, e1, b2, e2)`	returns an iterator where the second sequence is contained in the first, if it is not e1
`search (b1, e1, b2, e2, binp)`	as above, with a binary predicate binp used instead of equality

16.3.3 Mutating Sequence Algorithms

Mutating algorithms can modify the contents of the containers they work on. A typical operation is reversing the contents of a container.

In the following program the mutating library functions reverse() and copy() are used.

 Mutating Sequence Algorithm Program

In file stl_revr.cpp

```
//Use of mutating copy and reverse
#include <string>
#include <algorithm>
#include <vector>
using namespace std;

int main()
{
    string first_names[5] = { "laura", "ira", "buzz", "debra",
                               "twinkle" };
    string last_names[5] = { "pohl", "pohl", "dolsberry",
                              "dolsberry", "star" };
    vector<string> names(first_names, first_names + 5);
    vector<string> names2(10);
    vector<string>::iterator p;

    copy(last_names, last_names + 5, names2.begin());
    copy(names.begin(), names.end(), names2.begin() + 5);
    reverse(names2.begin(), names2.end());
    for (p = names2.begin(); p != names2.end(); ++p)
       cout << *p <<'\t';
}
```

The first invocation of the mutating function copy() places last_names in the container vector names2. The second call to copy() copies in the first_names, which had been used in the construction of the vector names. The function reverse() reverses all the elements that are then printed out.

We present the library prototypes for mutating algorithms.

- ```
  template<class InputIter, class OutputIter>
  OutputIter copy(InputIter b1, InputIter e1, OutputIter b2);
  ```

  This is a copying algorithm over the elements b1 to e1. The copy is placed starting at b2. The position returned is the end of the copy.

- ```
  template<class BidiIter1, class BidiIter2>
  BidiIter2 copy_backward(BidiIter1 b1, BidiIter1 e1,
                          BidiIter2 b2);
  ```

  This is a copying algorithm over the elements b1 to e1. The copy is placed starting at b2. The copying runs backward from e1 into b2, which are also going backward. The position returned is b2 - (e1 - b1).

- ```
  template<class BidiIter>
  void BidiIter(BidiIter b, BidiIter e);
  ```

  This reverses in place the elements b to e.

- ```
  template<class BidiIter, class OutputIter>
  OutputIter reverse_copy(BidiIter b1, BidiIter e1,
                          OutputIter b2);
  ```

  This is a reverse copying algorithm over the elements b1 to e1. The copy in reverse is placed starting at b2. The copying runs backward from e1 into b2, which are also going backward. The position returned is b2 + (e1 - b1).

- ```
  template<class ForwIter>
  ForwardIter unique(ForwIter b, ForwIter e);
  ```

  The adjacent elements in the range b to e are erased. The position returned is the end of the resulting range.

- ```
  template<class ForwIter, class BinaryPred>
  ForwardIter unique(ForwIter b, ForwIter e, BinaryPred bp);
  ```

  The adjacent elements in the range b to e with binary predicate bp satisfied are erased. The position returned is the end of the resulting range.

- ```
  template<class InputIter, class OutputIter>
  OutputIter unique_copy(InputIter b1, InputIter e1,
                         OutputIter b2);
  ```

  ```
  template<class InputIter, class OutputIter, class BinaryPred>
  OutputIter unique_copy(InputIter b1, InputIter e1,
                         OutputIter b2, BinaryPred bp);
  ```

The results are copied to b2 with the original range unchanged.

The remaining library functions are described in the following tables.

STL Mutating Sequence Library Functions	
`swap(t1, t2)`	swaps t1 and t2
`iter_swap(b1, b2)`	swaps pointed to locations
`swap_range(b1, e1, b2)`	swaps elements from b1 to e1 with those starting at b2; returns b2 + (e1 - b1)
`transform(b1, e1, b2, op)`	using the unary operator op transforms the sequence b1 to e1, placing it at b2; returns the end of the output location
`transform(b1, e1, b2, b3, bop)`	uses the binary operator bop on the two sequences starting with b1 and b2 to produce the sequence b3; returns the end of the output location
`replace(b, e, t1, t2)`	replaces in the range b to e the value t1 by t2
`replace_if(b, e, p, t2)`	replaces in the range b to e, the elements satisfying the predicate p by t2
`replace_copy(b1, e1, b2, t1, t2)`	copies and replaces into b2 the range b1 to e1 with the value t1 replacing t2
`replace_copy_if(b1, e1, b2, p, t2)`	copies and replace into b2 the range b1 to e1 with the elements satisfying the predicate p replacing t2
`remove(b, e, t)`	removes elements of value t
`remove_if, remove_copy, remove_copy_if`	similar to replace family except that values are removed
  ```

STL Mutating Sequence Library Functions	
fill(b, e, t)	assigns t to the range b to e
fill_n(b, n, t)	assigns n ts starting at b
generate(b, e, gen)	assigns to the range b to e by calling generator gen
generate_n(b, n, gen)	assigns n values starting at b using gen
rotate(b, m, e)	rotates leftward the elements of the range b to e; element in position i ends up in position $(i + n - m) \% n$, where n is the size of the range, m is the midposition, and b is the first position
rotate_copy(b1, m, e1, b2)	as above, but copied to b2 with the original unchanged
random_shuffle(b, e)	shuffles the elements
random_shuffle(b, e, rand)	shuffles the elements using the supplied random number generator rand
partition(b, e, p)	the range b to e is partitioned to have all elements satisfying predicate p placed before those that do not satisfy p
stable_partition(b, e, p)	as above, but preserving relative order

16.3.4 Numerical Algorithms

Numerical algorithms include sums, inner product, and adjacent difference.

In the following program the numerical function accumulate() performs a vector summation, and inner_product() performs a vector inner product.

▣ Numerical Algorithm Program

In file stl_numr.cpp

```
//Vector accumulation and innerproduct
#include <iostream>
#include <numeric>
using namespace std;
```

```
int main()
{
    double v1[3] = { 1.0, 2.5, 4.6 },
           v2[3] = { 1.0, 2.0, -3.5 };
    double sum, inner_p;

    sum = accumulate(v1, v1 + 3, 0.0);
    inner_p = inner_product(v1, v1 + 3, v2, 0.0);
    cout << "sum = " << sum
         << ", product = " << inner_p << endl;
}
```

These functions behave as expected on numerical types where + and * are defined. The library prototypes for numerical algorithms are as follows.

- ```
  template<class InputIter, class T>
  T accumulate(InputIter b, InputIter e, T t);
  ```

  This is a standard accumulation algorithm whose sum is initially t. The successive elements from the range b to e are added to this sum.

- ```
  template<class InputIter, class T, class BinOp>
  T accumulate(InputIter b, InputIter e, T t, BinOp bop);
  ```

  This is an accumulation algorithm whose sum is initially t. The successive elements from the range b to e are summed with sum = bop(sum, element).

We will use a table to briefly list other algorithms and their purpose as found in this library.

STL Numerical Library Functions	
`inner_product(b1, e1, b2, t)`	returns the inner product from the two ranges starting with b1 and b2; this product is initialized to t, which is usually zero
`inner_product(b1,e1,b2,t,bop1,bop2)`	returns a generalized inner product using bop1 to sum and bop2 to multiply
`partial_sum(b1, e1, b2)`	produces a sequence starting at b2, that is the partial sum of terms from the range b1 to e1
`partial_sum(b1, e1, b2, bop)`	as above, using bop for summation
`adjacent_difference(b1, e1, b2)`	produces a sequence starting at b2, that is the adjacent difference of terms from the range b1 to e1
`adjacent_difference(b1, e1, b2, bop)`	as above, using bop for difference

16.4 Functions

It is useful to have function objects to further leverage the STL library. For example, many of the previous numerical functions had a built-in meaning using + or *, but also had a form in which user-provided binary operators could be passed in as arguments. Defined function objects can be found in *function* or built. Function objects are classes that have `operator()` defined. These are inlined and are compiled to produce efficient object code.

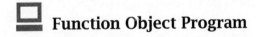 **Function Object Program**

In file stl_fucn.cpp

```
//Using a function object minus<int>
#include <iostream>
#include <numeric>
using namespace std;
```

```
int main()
{
    double v1[3] = { 1.0, 2.5, 4.6 }, sum;

    sum = accumulate(v1, v1 + 3, 0.0, minus<int>());
    cout << "sum = " << sum << endl;       //sum = -7
}
```

Accumulation is done using integer minus for the binary operation over the array v1[]. Therefore the double values are truncated, with the result being -7.

There are three defined function object classes.

STL Defined Function Object Classes

- Arithmetic objects
- Comparison objects
- Logical objects

We will use tables to briefly list algorithms and their purpose as found in this library.

STL Arithmetic Objects	
template <class T> struct plus<T>	adds two operands of type T
template <class T> struct minus<T>	subtracts two operands of type T
template <class T> struct times<T>	multiplies two operands of type T
template <class T> struct divides<T>	divides two operands of type T
template <class T> struct modulus<T>	modulus for two operands of type T
template <class T> struct negate<T>	unary minus for one argument of type T

Arithmetic objects are often used in numerical algorithms, such as accumulate().

STL Comparison Objects	
`template <class T>` `struct equal_to<T>`	equality of two operands of type T
`template <class T>` `struct not_equal_to<T>`	inequality of two operands of type T
`template <class T>` `struct greater<T>`	comparison by the greater (>) of two operands of type T
`template <class T>` `struct less<T>`	comparison by the less (<) of two operands of type T
`template <class T>` `struct greater_equal<T>`	comparison by the greater or equal (>=) of two operands of type T
`template <class T>` `struct less_equal<T>`	comparison by the lesser or equal (<=) of two operands of type T

The comparison objects are frequently used with sorting algorithms, such as `merge()`.

STL Logical Objects	
`template <class T> struct` `logical_and<T>`	performs logical and (&&) on two operands of type T
`template <class T>` `struct logical_or<T>`	performs logical or (||) on two operands of type T
`template <class T>` `struct logical_not<T>`	performs logical negation (!) on a single argument of type T

16.4.1 Function Adaptors

Function adaptors allow for the creation of function objects using adaption.

STL Function Adaptors

- Negators for negating predicate objects
- Binders for binding a function argument
- Adaptors for pointer to a function

In the following example we use a binder function bind2nd to transform an initial sequence of values to these values doubled.

Function Adaptor Program

In file stl_adap.cpp

```cpp
//Use of the function adaptor bind2nd
#include <iostream>
#include <algorithm>
#include <functional>
#include <string>
using namespace std;

template <class ForwIter>
void print(ForwIter first, ForwIter last, const char* title)
{
   cout << title << endl;
   while (first != last)
      cout << *first++ << '\t';
   cout << endl;
}

int main()
{
   int data[3] = { 9, 10, 11 };

   print(data, data + 3, "Original values");
   transform(data, data + 3, data, bind2nd(times<int>(), 2));
   print(data, data + 3, "New values");
}
```

We will use a table to briefly list algorithms and their purpose as found in this library.

STL Function Adaptors	

`template<class Pred>`
`unary_negate<Pred>`
`not1(const Pred& p)`
	returns `!p` where p is a unary predicate

`template<class Pred>`
`binary_negate<Pred>`
`not2(const Pred& p)`
	returns `!p` where p is a binary predicate

`template<class Op, class T>`
`binder1st<Op>bind1st`
`    (const Op& op,const T& t)`
	the binary op has a first argument bound to t; a function object is returned

`template<class Op, class T>`
`binder2nd<Op>bind2nd`
`    (const Op& op,const T& t)`
	the binary op has a second argument bound to t; a function object is returned

`template<class Arg,class T>` `ptr_fun(T (*f)(Arg))`	constructs a `pointer_to_unary_function<Arg, T>`

`template<class Arg1,`
`    class Arg2, class T>`
`ptr_fun(T (*f)(Arg1, Arg2))`
	constructs a `pointer_to_binary_function<Arg,T>`

16.5 Allocators

Allocator objects manage memory for containers. They allow implementations to be tailored to local system conditions while maintaining a portable interface for the container class.

Allocator definitions include: `value_type`, `reference`, `size_type`, `pointer`, and `difference_type`.

We will use a table to briefly list allocator member functions and their purpose as found in this library.

STL Allocator Members	
allocator(); ~allocator();	constructor and destructor for allocators
pointer address(reference r);	returns the address of r
pointer allocate(size_type n);	allocates memory for n objects of size_type from free store
void deallocate(pointer p);	deallocates memory associated with p
size_type max_size();	returns the largest value for difference_type; in effect, the largest number of element allo-catable to a container

Check your vendor's product for specific system-dependent implementations.

 ## Dr. P's Prescriptions: STL

- Program in a style compatible with STL.
- Use iterator parameters rather than container variables.
- Use the weakest iterator category compatible with the function.
- Use the most efficient container for a computation.
- Use vectors in place of native array types.

Prescription Discussion

STL augers a profound change in the programming habits of the C++ community. It introduces a library that promotes, without loss in efficiency, highly reusable, complex components. It is written to be general and efficient. It is orthogonal by design, in order that its various components can be maximally used with each other. Much of its value comes from its consistency. This enables the STL-aware programmer to easily understand and code STL-style components. For example, most STL generic functions work on input specified as an iterator range. This allows code to work on ordinary arrays where array addresses are passed in or to work on arbitrary STL containers. Another example is how STL frequently provides both a routine, such as unique(), that mutates data in place, and a second function, unique_copy(), that copies the mutated data.

Using iterator ranges for function parameters is more flexible than using container variables. A range can be use to extract a subset of a containers elements, and it is compatible with instantiation by array addresses. Designate, by choice of identifier name for the template variable, a weakest iterator type that solves the problem efficiently, so where possible, use input iterators. Resort to random access iterators only where this property is required by the algorithm. This leads to the most general and hence the most reusable code.

For any problem that requires a sequence container, any sequence container might be used. Learn the reasons for preferring one over another. For example, vector is preferred where random access is desirable. List is preferred when there is a lot of interior adding and deleting of elements. In many cases the choice is a compromise.

The native array and the STL vector are similiar in abilities and can frequently be used interchangeably. Native arrays can have efficiency advantages requiring less time and space resources. In most software this advantage is insignificant. The vector is more general allowing ready expendability and a general set of member functions for ease of use. Using vectors in place of arrays allows more robust, general and reusable code to be written.

Chapter 17

String Library

C++ provides a string type by including the standard header file *string*. It is the instantiation of a template class `basic_string<T>` with `char`. The string type provides member functions and operators that perform string manipulations, such as concatenation, assignment, or replacement. An example of a program using the string type for simple string manipulation follows.

String Library Program

In file stringt.cpp

```cpp
//String class to rewrite a sentence
#include <iostream>
#include <string>
using namespace std;

int main()
{
    string sentence, words[10];
    int pos = 0, old_pos = 0, nwords, i = 0;

    sentence = "Eskimos have 23 ways to ";
    sentence += "describe snow";
```

```
    while (pos < sentence.size()) {
        pos = sentence.find(' ', old_pos);
        words[i++].assign(sentence, old_pos, pos - old_pos);
        cout << words[i - 1] << endl;              //print words
        old_pos = pos + 1;
    }
    nwords = i;
    sentence = "C++ programmers ";
    for (i = 1; i < nwords -1; ++i)
        sentence += words[i] + ' ';
    sentence += "windows";
    cout << sentence << endl;
}
```

The string type is used to capture each word from an initial sentence where the words are separated by the space character. The position of the space characters is computed by the find() member function. Then the assign() member function is used to select a substring from sentence. Finally, a new sentence is constructed using the overloaded assignment, operator+=() and operator+() functions to perform assignments and concatenations.

We will describe the representation for a string of characters. It is also usual to have the instantiation basic_string<wchar_t> for a wide string type wstring. Other instantiations are possible as well.

String Private Data Members	
char* ptr	for pointing at the initial character
size_t len	for the length of the string
size_t res	for the currently allocated size, or for an unallocated string its maximum size

This implementation provides an explicit variable to track the string length, thus string length can be looked up in constant time, which is efficient for many string computations.

17.1 Constructors

Strings have seven public constructors, which makes it easy to declare and initialize strings from a wide range of parameters. Two of these provide conversions; namely a constructor on char* and a constructor on vector<char>.

String Constructor Members	
string()	default, creates an empty string.
string(const char* p)	conversion constructor from a pointer to char
string(const vector<char>& v)	conversion constructor from the vector container
string(const string& str, size_t pos = 0, size_t n = npos)	copy constructor; npos is usually −1 and indicates no memory was allocated
string(size_t size, capacity cap)	a string of '\0' is constructed of size where capacity is an enumeration type whose enumerator is default_size; otherwise a string of length zero is constructed
string(const char* p, size_t n)	copy n characters where p is the base address
string(char c, size_t n = 1)	construct a string of n cs

These constructors make it quite easy to use the string type initialized from char* pointers, which was the traditional C method for working with strings. Also, many computations are readily handled as a vector of characters. This is also facilitated by the string interface.

17.2 Member Functions

Strings have some members that overload operators, as briefly described in the next table.

String Overloaded Operator Members	
`string& operator=(const string& s)`	assignment operator
`string& operator=(const char* p)`	assigns a char* to a string
`string& operator=(const char c)`	assigns a char c to a string
`string& operator+=(const string&s)`	appends string s
`string& operator+=(const char* p)`	appends a char* to a string
`string& operator+=(const char c)`	appends a char c to a string
`operator vector<char>()const`	converts a string to a vector
`char operator[](size_t pos) const`	returns the character at pos
`char& operator[](size_t pos)`	returns the reference to the character at pos

There is an extensive set of public member functions that let you manipulate strings. In many cases these are overloaded to work with `string`, `char*`, and `char`. We will start by describing `append()`.

- `string& append(const string& s, size_t pos = 0, size_t n=npos);`

  Appends n characters starting at pos from s to the implicit string object.

  ```
  //example s1 "I am " s2 "7 years old"
  s1.append(s2);                  // s1 " I am 7 years old"
  s2.append(s1,0,4);              //s2 "7 years old I am"
  ```

- `string& append(const char* p, size_t n);`
  `string& append(const char* p);`
  `string& append(char c, size_t n = 1);`

  In each case a `string` object is constructed using the constructor of the same signature and appended to the implicit `string` object.

- `string& assign(const string& s, size_t pos = 0, size_t n=npos);`

  Assigns n characters starting at pos from s to the implicit string object.

  ```
  //example s1 " I am " s2 "7 years old"
  s1.assign(s2);                    // s1 "7 years old"
  ```

  The following signatures with the expected semantics are also overloaded:

  ```
  string& assign(const char* p, size_t n);
  string& assign(const char* p);
  string& assign(char c, size_t n = 1);
  ```

- `string& insert(size_t pos1, const string& str, size_t pos2 = 0,`
  `            size_t n = npos);`

  The insert() function is an overloaded set of definitions that insert a string of characters at a specified position. It inserts n characters taken from str, starting with pos2, into the implicit string at position pos1.

  ```
  //example s1 " I am " s2 " 7 years old"
  s1.insert(2,s2);                  // s1 "I 7 years old am"
  ```

The following signatures with the expected semantics are also overloaded:

```
string& insert(size_t pos,const char* p, size_t n);
string& insert(size_t pos, const char* p);
string& insert(size_t pos, char c, size_t n = 1);
```

The inverse function is remove().

- `string& remove(size_t pos = 0, size_t n = npos);`

  n characters are removed from the implicit string at position pos.

In the following table, we briefly describe further public string member functions.

String Members	
`string& replace(pos1, n1, str,` `pos2 = 0, n2 = npos)`	replaces at `pos1` for `n1` characters, the substring in `str` at `pos2` of `n2` characters

`string& replace(pos,n,p,n2);`
`string& replace(pos,n,p);`
`string& replace(pos,n,c,rep = 1);`
	replaces n characters at `pos`, using a `char* p` of `n2` characters, or a `char* p` until null, or a character c repeated `rep` times

`char get_at(pos) const;`	returns character in position `pos`
`void put_at(pos, c);`	places c at position `pos`
`size_t length() const;`	returns the string length
`const char* c_str() const;`	converts string to traditional `char*` representation
`const char* data() const;`	returns base address of the string representation
`void resize(n, c);` `void resize(n);`	resizes the string to length n; the padding character c is used in the first function and the `eos()` character is used in the second
`void reserve(size_t res_arg);` `size_t reserve() const;`	returns the private member `res`; the first function resets this
`size_t copy(p, n, pos=0) const;`	the implicit string starting at `pos` is copied into the `char* p` for n characters
`string substr(pos=0, n=npos)const;`	a substring of n characters of the implicit string is returned

You can lexicographically compare two strings using a family of overloaded member functions `compare()`.

- ```
  int compare(const string& str, size_t pos = 0,
              size_t n = npos) const;
  ```

Compares the implicit string starting at `pos` for n characters with `str`. Returns zero if the strings are equal; otherwise returns a positive or negative integer value indicating that the implicit string is greater or less than `str` lexicographically. The following signatures with the expected semantics are also overloaded:
  ```

```
int compare(const char* p,size_t pos, size_t n) const;
int compare(const char* p, size_t pos) const;
int compare(char c,size_t pos, size_t rep = 1) const;
```

Each signature specifies how the explicit string is constructed and then compared to the implicit string.

The final set of member functions perform a find operation. We will discuss one group and then summarize in a table the rest of this group of member functions.

- `size_t find(const string& str, size_t pos=0) const;`

The string `str` is searched for in the implicit string starting at `pos`. If it is found the position it is found at is returned; otherwise `npos` is returned, indicating failure.

The following signatures with the expected semantics are also overloaded:

```
size_t find(const char* p, size_t pos, size_t n)const;
size_t find(const char* p, size_t pos= 0) const;
size_t find(char c, size_t pos = 0) const;
```

Each signature specifies how the explicit string is constructed and then searched for in the implicit string. Further functions for finding strings and characters are briefly described in the following table.

String Find Members	

```size_t rfind(str, pos=npos) const;```
```size_t rfind(p, pos, n) const;```
```size_t rfind(p, pos=npos) const;```
```size_t rfind(c, pos=npos) const;```
	like `find()`, but scans the string backward for a first match

```size_t find_first_of```
```   (str, pos = 0) const;```
```size_t find_first_of```
```   (p, pos, n) const;```
```size_t find_first_of```
```   (p, pos=0) const;```
```size_t find_first_of```
```   (c,pos = 0) const;```
	searches for the first character of any character in the specified pattern, either `str`, `char* p`, or `char c`

```size_t find_last_of```
```   (str, pos = npos) const;```
```size_t find_last_of```
```   (p, pos, n) const;```
```size_t find_last_of```
```   (p, pos= npos) const;```
```size_t find_last_of```
```   (c,pos = npos) const;```
	searches backward for the first character of any character in the specified pattern, either `str`, `char* p`, or `char c`

```size_t find_first_not_of```
```   (str, pos = 0) const;```
```size_t find_first_not_of```
```   (p, pos, n) const;```
```size_t find_first_not_of```
```   (p, pos=0) const;```
```size_t find_first_not_of```
```   (c,pos = 0) const;```
	searches for the first character that does not match any character in the specified pattern, either `str`, `char* p`, or `char c`

```size_t find_last_not_of```
```   (str, pos = npos) const;```
```size_t find_last_not_of```
```   (p, pos, n) const;```
```size_t find_last_not_of```
```   (p, pos= npos) const;```
```size_t find_last_not_of```
```   (c,pos = npos) const;```
	searches backward for the first character that does not match any character in the specified pattern, either `str`, `char* p`, or `char c`

17.3 Global Operators

The string package contains operator overloadings that provide input/output, concatenation, and comparison operators. These are intuitively understandable and are briefly described in the following table.

String Overloaded Global Operators	
`ostream& operator<<(ostream& o,` `                    const string& s);`	output operator
`istream& operator>>(istream& in,` `                    string& s);`	input operator
`string operator+(const string& s1,` `                 const string& s2);`	concatenate s1 and s2
`bool operator==(const string& s1,` `                const string& s2);`	true if string s1 and s2 are lexicographically equal
`<   <=   >   >=   !=`	as expected

The comparison operators and the concatenation `operator+()` are also overloaded with the following four signatures:

```
bool operator==(const char* p, const string& s);
bool operator==(char c, const string& s);
bool operator==(const string& s, const char* p);
bool operator==(const string& s, char c);
```

In effect, a comparison or concatenation of any kind can occur between string and a second argument that is either a string, a character, or a character pointer.

 Dr. P's Prescriptions: String Library

■ Prefer the C++ standard library replacements to the C library.

■ As a corollary to the above `string` is preferred to `char*`.

Prescription Discussion

The new ANSI standard distinguishes old C libraries with names that start with "c" as in *cstdio* or *cstring*. In most cases, this is to allow older code to continue to work. Newer libraries used for the same purposes reflect important improvements. The `string` type found in the standard library header file *string* improves on `char*` in several ways. It has a richer set of operations and a more general interface. It can be more efficient because string lengths need not be recomputed. It is more robust because it provides better encapsulation and is not prone to memory leaks and address errors.

Chapter 18

Caution and Compatibility

C++ is not completely upward compatible with C. In most cases of ordinary use, it is a superset of C. Also, C++ is not a completely stable language design. It is in the process of being standardized. The following sections note features of the language that are problematic (reference DE 94).

18.1 Nested Class Declarations

The original scoping of nested classes was based on C rules. In effect, nesting was cosmetic, with the inner class globally visible. In C++, the inner class is local to the outer class enclosing it. Accessing such an inner class could require multiple uses of the scope resolution operator.

```
int outer::inner::foo(double w)      //foo is nested
    .....
```

It is also possible to have classes nested inside functions.

18.2 Type Compatibilities

In general, C++ is more strongly typed than ANSI C. Some differences are given in the following list.

Type Differences for ANSI C

- Enumerations are distinct types, with enumerators not being explicitly `int`. This means that enumerations must be cast when making assignments from integer types or other enumerations. Enumerations are promotable to integer. (See Chapter 3, "Constants," on page 11.)

- Any pointer type can be converted to a generic pointer of type `void*`. However, unlike in ANSI C, in C++ a generic pointer is not assignment-compatible with an arbitrary pointer type. This means that C++ requires that generic pointers be cast to an explicit type for assignment to a nongeneric pointer variable. (See Chapter 7, "Conversion Rules and Casts," on page 28.)

- A character constant in C++ is a `char`, but in ANSI C it is an `int`. The `char` type is distinct from both `signed char` and `unsigned char`. Functions may be overloaded based on the distinctions, and pointers to the three types are not compatible.

18.3 Miscellaneous

The old C function syntax, where the argument list is left blank, is replaced in ANSI C by the explicit argument `void`. The signature `foo()` in C is considered equivalent to the use of ellipses, and in C++ is considered equivalent to the empty argument list.

In early C++ systems, the `this` pointer could be modified. It could be used to allocate memory for class objects. Although this use is obsolete, a compiler can continue to allow it. (See Section 11.4, "The this Pointer," on page 80.)

C++ allows declarations to be intermixed with executable statements. ANSI C allows declarations to be at the heads of blocks or in file scope only. However, in C++, `goto`, iteration, and selection statements are not allowed to bypass initialization of variables. This rule differs from ANSI C.

In C++, a global data object must have exactly one definition. Other declarations must use the keyword `extern`. ANSI C allows multiple declarations without the keyword `extern`.

Chapter 19

New Features in C++

Most compilers have complete implementations of templates and exceptions. The behavior of new with exceptions implemented is to throw an xalloc or bad_alloc exception. (See Chapter 14, "Exceptions," on page 113.)

Mechanisms that dynamically determine object type have entered the language. This is called run-time type identification (RTTI). The new operator typeid() applied to either a *type-name* or an *expression* and dynamic_cast<t*ype*>(*pointer*), whose effect is either to return zero if the cast fails or to perform the cast. With exceptions in use, the standard library bad_cast exception is thrown when a conversion fails. In general, such casts will be allowed in polymorphic class hierarchies. (See Section 12.5, "Run-Time Type Identification," on page 95.)

Also added are cast conversion operators, static_cast and reinterpret_cast. (See Chapter 7, "Conversion Rules and Casts," on page 27.)

Single-argument constructors may be prohibited from being conversion constructors with the use of the keyword explicit. (See Section 11.1, "Constructors and Destructors," on page 73.)

The keyword mutable allows data members of class variables that have been declared const to remain modifiable. (See Section 11.7, "Mutable," on page 86.)

Two new types, bool and wchar_t, were added to the simple types. (See Chapter 6, "Types," on page 23.)

The existence of libraries that can lead to name clashes motivated the additional of a namespace scope. (See Section 4.1, "Namespaces," on page 16.) The standard library is encapsulated in the namespace std. This library includes the standard container classes, iterators, and algorithms of the STL library.

See system manuals for a detailed description of what is implemented.

Chapter 20

References

- ABC 95
  Kelley, A., and Pohl, I., *A Book on C, Third Edition*. 1995. Reading, MA: Addison-Wesley.

- ARM 90
  Ellis, M., and Stroustrup, B., *The Annotated C++ Reference Manual*. 1990. Reading, MA: Addison-Wesley.

- C4C 94
  Pohl, I., *C++ for C Programmers, Second Edition*. 1994. Reading, MA: Addison-Wesley.

- C4P 95
  Pohl, I., *C++ for Pascal Programmers, Second Edition*. 1995. Reading, MA: Addison-Wesley.

- DE 94
  Stroustrup, B., *The Design and Evolution of C++*. 1994. Reading, MA: Addison-Wesley.

- DP 95
  Gamma, E., Helm, R., Johnson, R., and Vlissides, J., *Design Patterns: Elements of Reusable Object-Oriented Software*. 1995. Reading, MA: Addison-Wesley.

- EC 92
  Meyers, S., *Effective C++: 50 Specific Ways to Improve your Programs and Designs*. 1992. Reading, MA: Addison-Wesley.

- GRAY 91
  Stroustrup, B., *The C++ Programming Language, Second Edition*. 1991. Reading, MA: Addison-Wesley.

- IOS 93
  Teale, S., *C++ IO Streams Handbook.* 1993. Reading, MA: Addison-Wesley.

- KR 88
  Kernighan, B., and Ritchie, D., *The C Programming Language, Second Edition.* 1988. Englewood Cliffs, NJ: Prentice Hall.

- KP 74
  Kernighan, B., and Plauger, P., *The Elements of Programming Style.* 1974. New York, NY: McGraw-Hill.

- LIP 91
  Lippman, S., *The C++ Primer, Second Edition.* 1991. Reading, MA: Addison-Wesley.

- OOAD 94
  Booch, G., *Object-Oriented Analysis and Design, Second Edition.* 1995. Reading, MA: Addison-Wesley.

- OPUS 97
  Pohl, I., *Object-Oriented Programming Using C++, Second Edition.* 1997. Reading, MA: Addison-Wesley.

- STL 96
  Musser, D. and Saini, A., *STL Tutorial and Reference Guide: C++ Programming with the Standard Template Library.* 1996. Reading, MA: Addison-Wesley.

- STLP 96
  Glass, G. and Schuchert, B., *The STL <Primer>.* 1996. Upper Saddle River, NJ: Prentice Hall.

- TG 94
  Taligent Inc., *Taligent's Guide to Designing Programs: Well-Mannered Object-Orietned Design in C++.* 1994. Reading, MA: Addison-Wesley.

Index

W

X

Z